Complete LinkedIn Marketing, Branding and Advertising Social Media Guide

Comprehensive Step by Step Guide for creating LinkedIn Advertising, Generating Sales Leads and Develop a Personal Brand

Chris J. Brodie

© Copyright 2019 - All rights reserved.

The author or the publisher of this book gives no one the right to reproduce, duplicate, or transmit the knowledge contained herein without due permission.

Neither the author nor publisher is accountable for any damages, reparation, or monetary loss as a result of the information contained in this book.

Legal Notice:

This book is only for personal use. You cannot amend, distribute, sell, use, quote or paraphrase any part, or the content within this book without the consent of the author or publisher.

Disclaimer:

The information contained in this book has been documented for educational and entertainment purposes. While all effort was put into providing detailed and up-to-date information, no warranty of any nature is declared.

Also, the author does not in any way push forward any legal, financial, or professional advice. The content of this book has been gathered from different sources, so consult a licensed professional before you adopt any technique outlined herein.

Table of Contents

Introduction 10
Chapter 1: LinkedIn Basics 12
   What is LinkedIn? 12
   How Does LinkedIn Enable Networking? 13
   What is LinkedIn Used for? 13
      To Grow Your Network 13
      Join or Create a Forum 14
      To Create Opportunities 14
      To Grow Business Ventures 14
      Status Updates 14
      Blog 15
      To Build a Platform 15
      To Locate Your Tribe 15
      Job Search 15
      For Following the Leaders 16
      Profiles Search 16
      Companies & Brands 16
      Individuals 16
   Basic Features Available on LinkedIn 16
   Resourceful Features for Everybody and Business 17
   Benefits of LinkedIn to your Marketing Strategy 19
      It Offers a Friendly Environment for Your Business to Thrive 19
      It Makes Discovering New Talent Easy 19
      It Enables Personal and Professional Credibility 19
      You Can Push Traffic to Your Site 20
      You Can Launch Products on LinkedIn 20

- It Aids Meaningful Professional Relationships 20
- It Boosts Brand's Visibility 20
- You Can Use LinkedIn Posts to Get to all your Page's Followers 21

Chapter 2: How Can You Create LinkedIn Account? 22
- Guides to Setting up a LinkedIn Login 22
  - Step 1 22
  - Step 2 22
  - Step 3 23
- How Do You Create A LinkedIn Company Account? 24
  - Step 1 24
  - Step 2 25
  - Step 3 25
  - Step 4 26
  - Step 5 26
  - Step 6 26
  - Step 7 26
  - Step 8: Content Creation 27
- LinkedIn Premium Account 27
  - Recruiter Lite: 28
  - Job Seeker: 28
  - Business Plus: 29
  - Sales Navigator: 29
- How To Make Payment For Premium Account 29

Chapter 3: How to Create a LinkedIn Profile That Sells 31
- Vital Characteristics of a LinkedIn profile 31
- Does A Good Profile Influence Sales? 32
  - Build Your Profile Through The Eyes of the Buyers 32
  - Incorporate a Stunning Headshot Photo 33
  - Create a Great Headline 33
  - Make Your Profile Summary Compelling 34

Your Use of English is a Criteria	35
Include Media	35
Optimize the Experience Section	35
Understand Your Company's Policies	36
Leave no Field Untouched	36
Standard Profile Is Important to the Success of Your Sales	37
Chapter 4: Determining Your Ideal Customers	**38**
Create A Profile of Your Ideal Client	38
Add them together	39
Identify Your Collaborators – Companies or Individuals	39
How Do You Establish Connection?	39
Identify Ideal Customers Using Area(s) of Shared Interest	40
Path to Successfully Marketing to Your Ideal Clients	40
How Do You Find Your Niche on LinkedIn?	41
How to Identify Your Niche On LinkedIn	41
Follow Thought-leaders in Your Industry	41
Use Targeted Keywords to Discover Specific Niche-Relevant Groups	42
Try Direct Connections	42
Chapter 5: Best LinkedIn practices	**43**
Are LinkedIn Best Practices Necessary?	43
Determine Your Type of Content	43
Encourage Your Staff Members to Post Brand-Content	46
Optimize LinkedIn Pulse	46
Remain Active	47
Use LinkedIn Analytics to Track Your Success	48
Getting More Results Using LinkedIn	48
LinkedIn Mistakes That You Should Avoid	48
Not Creating Thorough Goals	49
Your Profile Does Not Pronounce Your Expertise	49
You Share Too Personal Events	50

- Not Improving Your LinkedIn 50
- Neglecting Your Network 51
- Forgetting Keywords 51
- Not Requesting for Help 51

Chapter 6: Creating the Content That Attracts on LinkedIn 52
- Blogs 52
- Images 53
- Infographics 54
- White Papers and Case Studies 54
- Video 55
- Webinars 55
- Podcasts and Audio 56
- Downloadables 56

Factors To Consider Before Choosing Your Type of Content 56
Effective use of Content Marketing 57
Guide For LinkedIn Content Marketing Plan 57
Focus on Your Network Growth 58
- Creation of Company Page 59
- Focused Content Marketing 59
- Create a Plan that is Specific to the Newsfeed 60
- Be Selective with Groups Membership 61
- Keep Personal Thoughts To Yourself 61
- Learn Patience 61
- Schedule Your Updates 62
- Keep it straight and short 62
- Getting Headlining Right 62
- Be Consistent 62
- Optimize LinkedIn Publishing Platform 63
- Incorporate the Use of SlideShare 63

Chapter 7: How to Boost Your Connections 64

- Degrees of LinkedIn Connection ... 64
- Is Having a Large Network Significant? ... 65
- Who Are the People to Connect With? ... 66
  - Professionals You Are Familiar With ... 66
  - Professionals You Love to Meet or Know ... 66
  - Family, Friends and Acquaintances ... 66
  - Those with Many Connections ... 66
  - Those with Prospects ... 67
  - Those with Attractive Skills ... 67
  - Your Consistent Critic ... 67
  - Design Your Connection Requests ... 67
  - Connect With Those You Meet Physically ... 68
  - Set Goals ... 68
  - Post Content Each Day ... 68
  - Include your LinkedIn profile URL in your Email Signature ... 69
  - Join groups ... 69
  - Input Keywords in Your profile ... 70
  - Share Relevant Content on LinkedIn's Publishing Platform ... 70
  - Use Images ... 70
  - Keep Engaging Your Present Connections ... 70
  - Leverage Other Social Platforms in Promoting Your LinkedIn URL ... 71
  - Make Use of your Email Contacts ... 71
  - Send Connect Requests to LIONS ... 71
  - Connect with Individuals Who Check Out Your Profile ... 72
  - Publish Videos ... 72
- **Chapter 8: Steps to Creating Successful Ads on LinkedIn** ... 73
  - How does LinkedIn Ads Work? ... 73
  - Developing Your Campaign ... 73
    - Pick your objective ... 73
    - Select Your Target Audience ... 74

- Determine the Ad Format 75
- Placement 76
- Ascertain your Budget & Schedule 76
  - Budget 76
  - Schedule 77
  - Type of Bid 77
  - Tracking Your Conversions 78
  - Building Up Your Ad(s) 78
  - Include a CTA (Call-to-Action) 79
  - Give Value 79
  - Testing 79
- Evaluating your LinkedIn Ad Campaign 80
- Optimizing Your Ad Campaigns 80
  - Check the CTR of Ad Campaign 80
  - Change a Variable 80
  - Frequently Update your Audience Attributes 80
- Measuring Your Ad leads using Post-Click Reporting 81

Chapter 9: Guide to Creating a LinkedIn Marketing Funnel 82
- Funnels: What You Should Know 82
- Stages of a Funnel 82
  - Step 1: Identify Your Prospects and Connect 83
  - Send a Personalized Request to Connect 84
  - Step 2: Engage and Develop a Relationship with your Connections 84
  - Step 3: Give Value & Build Trust 84
  - Step 4: Strengthen Relationships 85
  - Step 5: Engage in Conversation Offline 86

Chapter 10: Important Tools and Apps to Optimize 87
- LinkedIn Sales Navigator 87
- Webfluential 88
- LinkedIn Plugins 88

- eLink Pro ... 89
- Crystal ... 89
- LeadGrabber Pro ... 89
- Dux-Soup ... 90
- LinkedIn Small Business ... 90
- LeadFuze ... 90
- Outro ... 91
- Salestools.io ... 91
- Discoverly ... 92
- Rapportive ... 92
- LinkedIn Elevate ... 93
- Guru ... 93
- SalesLoft ... 93
- Voogy ... 94
- LinkedIn Marketing Tools: Making Use of the Best Option(s) ... 94
- Using Tools Appropriately ... 94
  - Using LinkedIn Tools To Build Compound Connection ... 94
  - Being Permanently Restricted Is Rare but Beware ... 95
  - Approved In-house Practices for LinkedIn Tools ... 95
  - Effective Tools Act Like the Real User ... 95
  - Tools Don't Offer the Same Functionalities ... 96
  - Be Resourceful ... 96
- Circumventing LinkedIn Usage Limits ... 97
- When Tools On LinkedIn Is Not Necessary ... 97

Conclusion ... 98
Bibliographies ... 99

Introduction

LinkedIn is such a popular word that goes around yet it shouldn't be a surprise that quite a number of people are yet to grab whatever it is the platform represents. We bet you must have heard from friends and acquaintances. Someone had once said LinkedIn is a platform he doesn't think he would be able to make sense of. But really, is LinkedIn that technical?

So, what is LinkedIn?

LinkedIn is a social platform which has been designed for professionals. Perhaps, the reason most find it difficult to embrace is that unlike other social media platforms like Facebook, LinkedIn focuses more on your career perspectives. Thus, if you are intentional and serious about building your career, it's time to take LinkedIn serious.

Intro to the LinkedIn Platform

Is LinkedIn for everyone? Yes. Irrespective of your position – a freshman in college, a job seeker, a marketing expert in a multinational company, you need LinkedIn in order to take your career to the next height. It should be emphasized that LinkedIn offers a wide opportunity for growth and professional connections for anyone who is ready to tap into it.

Can you then conclude that it's a networking platform? Looking at the manner of LinkedIn, we can say YES. It's an opportunity to interact with leaders and professionals in various industries. You can share contacts and business cards with them via the same virtual space. Eventually, a lot of opportunities abound to meet them physically or get referred through them for job placements and others.

However, instead of friends and followers on Facebook and Twitter respectively, LinkedIn allows you to relate with others through what is called "connections". Each connection refers to a user that you add to your network. Once you are connected, you will be able to see and follow their posts and career. Beyond that, through the contact information available on their profile or via private message feature, you can start a meaningful conversation. But then, you must have set up your profile on the platform, showcase your experience and successes in the most professional way possible. Doing this will help you attract like-minded individuals like you or above you. Don't forget that it all starts with how you present yourself.

Is there any similarity between LinkedIn and Facebook? With respect to features and layout, we can say that with a good knowledge of how Facebook works, it becomes easier to navigate on LinkedIn. It is quite similar to Facebook when you look at their general features and layout. The only striking difference is the focus on professionals.

The chapters to follow will contain a lot of information that will make you an expert in using LinkedIn, so you can further progress your career. For instance, you will learn all about LinkedIn, how to setup a profile and page for your company, LinkedIn's importance to brand exposure, and so on. The chapters will also contain information that will help you generate more connections, create ads, etc.

Chapter 1:
LinkedIn Basics

On a general note, the evolution of social media has opened new opportunities for advertising and promotion of business to professionals. In the same vein, it has helped most business owners and professionals to understand how these platforms work. At least, basic knowledge is required. However, it must be said that unlike Facebook, Twitter, and Instagram, LinkedIn has not been used optimally.

This is really something to worry about especially as it is the best platform for B2B marketers to thrive. Interestingly, it is the perfect platform suitable for B2B marketers. It is for its high prospect that it was acquired by Microsoft for $26billion.

After a careful study of the platform and the manner with which newcomers utilize it, one thing is common – most users create profile which does not bring them significant return. This could be linked to the seeming complexity of the platform in part or the sheer disinterest of the users in spending time to create a professionally interesting profile.

Yet, irrespective of the seeming complexity, it cannot be denied that LinkedIn remains one of the important digital resources which anyone must have. Yes, a must-have, if you intend to take your career to a greater height.

So, if you are not on the platform yet or if your LinkedIn account is dormant, now is the time to get serious. Are you ready to know more about this amazing social network for business and professionals? Let's get started.

What is LinkedIn?

LinkedIn has about 610 million users, and that's really low for an online network that's described as the leading platform for professionals.

Please note that the number keeps increasing daily. In fact, professionals are joining the platform at a rate of two persons per seconds. And these users are distributed across about 200 countries of the world. Among these users are people in various jobs, professions, arts, and industries. As you can see, it's a very wide platform where you can tap into multiple opportunities.

To a larger extent, LinkedIn has led to a revolution about how social media marketing and content marketing operations can be executed. Presentation is key especially if you are a job seeker or trying to explore new fields, making attempt to boost your visibility or your social network.

LinkedIn opens up a beautiful channel for you to seek employment, stay connected with professionals in the field, and recruit competent talent. Whatever field you are in, if you want to progress in this digital age, you have no excuse not to be on LinkedIn.

How Does LinkedIn Enable Networking?

We can liken LinkedIn to a mixer, virtually though. It allows you to connect with people that you know or intend to know. In this category are people on your phone contact or mail list. Irrespective of their numbers, LinkedIn allows you to connect with them.

But to establish a successful connection, you need to set up a good profile. And that's where most people get it wrong. Let's face it, LinkedIn is not as complex as we think it is. The one thing we have failed to do is the need to study how it works.

To build a good profile, ensure you make a compelling and accurate summary of yourself, including your profession – past, present, and future if need be. Please, never forget to state important points about yourself, your education, job experience, awards, and publications. And don't forget that no experience is unimportant.

Also, ensure that you upload a clear picture of yourself. Build your profile above average, you might not be a professional yet in your field but build a standard profile.

Above all else, be active. If you are on LinkedIn but inactive, you should be on your mark now. Your level of activeness has a lot to do with how fast you can become a personality to reckon with in your chosen industry.

How do you become active, you might want to ask? Post content that are useful to those in your market niche or industry. Comment and like posts of those you have connected with in your industry. Share what they say with others. Join a forum that can enable your need for growth and visibility. These are important to-dos because doing them consistently boost your growth level.

What is LinkedIn Used for?

To Grow Your Network

Network is important to any form of growth you want to experience in your field. Isn't that why conferences, seminars, and forums are now attended by professionals globally? And the truth is that you don't have to wait till you become a professional in your chosen field before you network.

LinkedIn offers anyone with interest a wide opportunity to grow and develop. You might be an expert networker or a newbie, as long as you are ready to take a chance, the ball is in your court. It only costs you good internet connection and a browsing phone, basically.

Join or Create a Forum

Like we said earlier, the striking difference between Facebook and LinkedIn is that the latter allows you to connect with professionals in your field. So, like what you are used to on Facebook, LinkedIn also gives you an opportunity to join a forum, group, network that interests you. Besides, you can also create your own if you believe in your own voice.

However, you should make sure that whatever group you join, there is mutual interest. Don't be silent on any group, participate in whatever they do and make sure that you contribute to discussions meaningfully.

To Create Opportunities

If you seek opportunities, LinkedIn is the right place to be. This is not to say other networks are not important. But if you are intentional about your growth in any field, LinkedIn is a platform that you should begin to take seriously. While you are seeking opportunities, there are top managers and professionals in industries who are on the platform to create opportunities. So, the opportunities that await you are so massive. When you are consistently active, your connections will be willing to refer you for opportunities while it won't be difficult for you to also seek.

To Grow Business Ventures

LinkedIn offers business owners and entrepreneurs various options to grow and expand their businesses. If your targets are other businesses, then LinkedIn is the right place to be. Let no one tell you otherwise. On LinkedIn, you can execute your marketing strategies like content marketing. Not only that, you can buy targeted ads while using tools offered by the platform to track the number of views, level of engagement, and reach at the same time.

Status Updates

Like it has been so far emphasized, consistency is key on LinkedIn. You have to be active and one of the things you do to stay active is updating status. If you want to build a standard profile, you will have to pay attention to posting informative and relevant content. It could be a short or long well-composed article about things you are passionate about. Don't forget that interest is key and make sure you have done your homework well before you post anything.

When it comes to staying active through consistent posting, another thing you should note is the need to respond when people react. Don't post and be gone. Respond to comments and questions. When your connections see that you acknowledge their voice, they will always be willing to react to whatever you post.

If the case is otherwise, you would be lucky to get 3likes when next you post on LinkedIn.

Blog

Do you have a flair for blogging, LinkedIn allows you to share what you write while you also have access to what others are blogging about. This is one of the best ways to establish yourself as a thought leader in your chosen field or any new field of interest you are targeting.

To Build a Platform

There is no restriction to what you can do on LinkedIn as long as it is professional. So, here is an opportunity to optimally use your passion.

LinkedIn allows you to build a platform where you can pass quality message across to your connections and followers. The tools are there for you to use.

To Locate Your Tribe

There is always a tribe for every field of interest. This is not about the ethnic group you belong to. The members of the tribe being referred to here are those who share the same value and interest with you.

Wouldn't it be fantastic to link up with them? Through the tribe, you get to know your network, expand your own knowledge as you learn from one another. The opportunities are large, the question is: which tribe do you want to be known with?

Job Search

Don't be surprised by the tons of job opportunities available on LinkedIn. While some are there to build their personal brand, a lot more are there to search for job opportunities. That's why it was stated from the start that you have to spend quality time on creating a profile that is standard. And don't forget that your profile includes your CV, resume, job experience, educational history, credentials, and awards, among others.

However, don't forget the need to be active and visible. People who have got job opportunities on LinkedIn didn't get it on a platter of gold. You have to be active and visible at first. So, don't just create a standard profile and go.

When you are active on your page and in platforms/tribes that you belong to, you have a great chance of being recommended and endorsed for jobs by any of your connections. One amazing thing is that when you are visible, the job opportunities that come your way may not be publicized on LinkedIn. People are watching after all, so if there is an opening in their company, they recommend you in-house.

For Following the Leaders

You want to hear from the leaders in industries, companies, and professions. They are human too who take time to share their thoughts and well-researched fact via LinkedIn posts to influence people like you who are interested in career growth. So, if becoming effective in your field of interest is a good deal to you, get on LinkedIn.

Profiles Search

You are looking to stay connected with leaders? Or targeting a particular group for your B2B/B2C marketing strategy, LinkedIn grants you search tools to do this. You can carry out a targeted search that helps you connect with the right the professionals and companies.

When you search through profiles, you are able to see their educational history, work experience, awards and publications, as well as present field of engagement.

Companies & Brands

There are companies and brands on LinkedIn. Not only can you find them and connect, you get to see their regular updates about their management, market research, and vacant positions, among others.

Individuals

There are also individuals on LinkedIn who have become personal brands. We can call them influencers or visionary leaders, right? It's common to see the "Influencer" badge on their profiles. Well, you too can get there.

Through the same platform, individuals who have attained this status are allowed, frequently, by LinkedIn to share blog posts, update status, and videos. You can always connect with them for to improve your career and business.

Basic Features Available on LinkedIn

Some of the basic features available on LinkedIn are examined below:

- Home: As soon you sign up and log in to the platform, you are ready to start making connections. Your newsfeed will then start to show you the activities of your connections. Remember that these includes individuals, professionals, and the pages of companies you are following.

- Profile: Once you have taken your time to create standard profile, this feature displays your name, location, picture, what you are engaged in, your educational history, among others. As you progress in your career, this feature also allows you to add or remove details.

- Jobs: Ton of jobs are posted by individuals, professionals, and companies each day. This feature allows you to see them. With your profile information as well as specific setting you have initiated on your profile, LinkedIn also recommends jobs to you.

- My Network: With this feature, you will see all the connections you have. To see other options that you can add to your contact, all you have to do is place the mouse over this feature and the options will pop-up.

- Search Bar: This is your search engine that allows you see massive results based on the field you are targeting. For more specific search for jobs, companies, and professionals, there is an *Advanced option* close to the search bar. This is a very reliable feature.

- Messages: This feature allows you to start a conversation with those you are connected with. This can be done through private messages. Pictures and documents can be attached through this.

- Notifications: Just like other social media platforms, LinkedIn notifies you when any of your connections sends you an invite to join a group, to read a post, or recommends you for something. This also includes invitation to connect by a professional or approval of your connection request with someone.

The above are basic features that you are privy to when you sign-up for a LinkedIn account. There are more advanced features which you need as a professional, but you have to upgrade to premium account before you can access them.

Resourceful Features for Everybody and Business

UNLIKE the basic features that you can access as soon as you open your LinkedIn account, there are other resources which can be used to professionally enhance the growth of everybody and business.

- LinkedIn Learning: When you are on the right platform, it's not hard to find answers to important questions concerning anything. That's the opportunity which LinkedIn learning offer.

Exceedingly, this feature allows you to search for software, skills, and programs that you are interested in. You really can't believe what awaits you until you navigate through to the LinkedIn learning home page.

Almost everything you are looking for has been placed under categories like trends, editor's picks, and learn within 30 minutes. If you want to keep your brain and mind sharp especially as it concerns your industry, LinkedIn learning home page is recommended.

- Active Status: Don't let your green dot be found wanting. Just like Facebook, LinkedIn offers you the same feature. At the page of your connections, you will always see the green dot beside the photo of those who are active.

The case is the same if you have set your active status to be seen. To turn it on, see the steps below:

1. Go to "Settings & Privacy" page beneath your photo.
2. On the privacy page, move downward till you find "How others see your LinkedIn activity."
3. Select "Manage active status."
4. And save the changes where applicable.

- Career Advice: thinking of a new career path, you can always get advice from professionals in that field via LinkedIn. In the same way, if you have need advice to give, you will eventually be connected to someone within your field of knowledge.

When you begin to use your knowledge and expertise to help others on LinkedIn, it wouldn't be long before you attract massive invitation to connect. Ultimately, you can use it as a form of online marketing.

- LinkedIn Publishing: While this feature has existed for a long time, many people failed to key into it. Not thanks to its seeming complication then. However, it has been made easier by LinkedIn. This is an opportunity for you to publish authentic content and with a simple change to the publishing settings, anyone who is not even on LinkedIn can view and read. What do you gain from reaching a wide range of users? Your gains include more business opportunities and connections, increased conversion rate for your business, and increased credibility as a thought-leaders. It's that easy.

- Advanced Search: Carrying out online searches could be daunting. This shouldn't be new if you love to shop online. But nothing to worry about here. LinkedIn offers you the opportunity to search professionally through its *Advanced search*. Just by adding filters, you control what shows up the moment you carry out a search query in the search bar.

Also, this feature allows you to be found easily by prospective clients. Meanwhile, this only works bets if your profile is complete. We will talk more about this in subsequent parts.

Now, let's consider some of the benefits brought to you by LinkedIn.

Benefits of LinkedIn to your Marketing Strategy

Whether you are managing a new business or it's been existent for a long time, a thorough marketing strategy is important. Unfortunately, an important resources which marketers ignore while mapping their marketing strategy is LinkedIn.

One thing they have failed to understand is that apart from doing all it takes to boost their client base and network, LinkedIn can connect them to professionals who can help their business attain success.

But then, you should be ready to run your account with skill and proficiency that are required for business success.

Apart from that, in what other ways can you benefit from creating a LinkedIn account and being active online? See them below.

It Offers a Friendly Environment for Your Business to Thrive

From inception, LinkedIn was designed for professionals and companies. Apart from that, its algorithm is not as complicated when compared to what obtains on other platforms like Facebook and Instagram. This has been made possible in order to ensure that your reach as an individual or business spreads through your groups online without jeopardizing the needed level of social connections.

Everything that your business needs to succeed in the virtual space is on LinkedIn.

It Makes Discovering New Talent Easy

In a research carried out by LinkedIn, social media sites have encountered about 72% boost in their use as job placement and recruitment platforms.

Until now, career platforms used to be the places where new talents could be discovered. The case is now quite different, thanks to the evolution of social media. Professional websites like LinkedIn can now be used to find new talents for recruitment into new and existing companies.

It Enables Personal and Professional Credibility

If you are seeking personal and professional credibility, you should be on LinkedIn. Many individuals and businesses are yet to take advantage of the opportunities offered by this platform. Now that you know, it's better than being late. Join now!

How can you take advantage of this unique opportunity?

- Stand out by posting content related to your market niche two or more times every week. If you can do this daily, please do.

- Make sure your content is always compelling.
- Be consistent. Never miss your routine twice.
- Use your business profile to upload posts in order to establish yourself as an expert.
- Also post on your profile so as to build a strong connection with your followers.
- Don't forget to be consistent.

You Can Push Traffic to Your Site

As long as you are consistently posting on your profile and you have the attention and interest of your followers and connections, you can begin to include links that will redirect them to your website for additional information.

Remember that you must have been posting consistently, gaining their trust before incorporating link building into your posting.

You Can Launch Products on LinkedIn

Professional social media platforms like LinkedIn can be used to launch products. Doing this will make a lot of impact than you can ever imagine. It needs not saying but it should be mentioned that sites like LinkedIn has changed the face of how product information can be shared. You don't even have to wait till the product gets to the market or distributors' stores. You can market first to other businesses and individuals who are your targets.

It Aids Meaningful Professional Relationships

With LinkedIn, you can build meaningful professional relationships. In addition, recent research suggests that it is a vital tool to fortifying physical connections.

It Boosts Brand's Visibility

A standard profile and fully optimized business page can help in *slightly* boosting your ranking on Google's search engine result pages (SERPs).

Please note the use of slightly because there are a lot of ranking factors that are put into consideration by the search engine before any page could rank at the top.

Still, no matter how little a well-optimized LinkedIn account could mean to Google ranking, you could imagine the difference it could make on your conversion rate.

In order to rank in the search results, note the following search engine optimization (SEO) strategies.

- Incorporate the right/premium keywords into your page bio and description.
- Use strong descriptive words in your page bio and description.
- Don't leave every necessary sections blank.
- Incorporate link building strategies by linking your blog and sites in your posts, profile, and descriptions.

You Can Use LinkedIn Posts to Get to all your Page's Followers

Unlike other platforms, LinkedIn posts have the highest possibility of getting to the feeds of all your followers. This is because there is no filtering of feed.

Whatever you post or update on your LinkedIn company's page, show up on their feeds automatically. That is if they are your followers. And it doesn't matter if they have had any form of engagement with your post recently or not.

So, when you update meaningful and useful posts, there is no worry about restriction. None of your audience is restricted by algorithm.

Meanwhile, we are not implying that everyone you are aiming to target on LinkedIn would be online when you post. To beat this, you need to be consistent with posting. That's just the way it is to winning with your content marketing effort on LinkedIn.

A 2014 study carried out by the Content Marketing Institute and MarketingProfs revealed that 94% of B2B marketers use LinkedIn for circulating content. Besides, these marketers ascribed the platform as the most effective when it comes to ranking on the top page of search results.

As you can see, there is nothing stopping you from winning.

Chapter 2:
How Can You Create LinkedIn Account?

To be a part of the LinkedIn community, you need to set up an account. This is a small price to pay when compared with the opportunities you stand to gain through connections and followership.

There is no other way to doing it- you need an account in order to grow a personal network.

In this chapter, we will be talking about simplified process that you need to follow to create a Log-in and Business account on LinkedIn.

Guides to Setting up a LinkedIn Login

This is intended to be a practical process. So, open your browser and go to LinkedIn.com. Then, follow the steps below to create your log-in details.

Step 1

Once you have been directed to the page of LinkedIn, navigate to the **Join Now Button** at the right side of the page. Click on it and you wait while you are directed to a page where you will be required to supply basic data in the boxes provided.

The requirements in the order of appearance are:

- First name
- Last name
- Email address
- A strong password with not less than six characters

How do you come up with strong password?

Coming up with a strong password -100/100, is not a complicated. Just know how to combine uppercase, lowercase, number, and some special character.

Step 2

Revealing information that concern your location and employment status are the actions you need to take in this step. The options available for you to pick from are:

- Employed

- Looking for Work
- Business Owner
- Working Independently
- A student

You should know that the option you pick would influence other fields that you would be required to fill. For example, if you picked *Employed* as your option, the other fields that would pop-up include company, country zip, code of your location, and job title as well as description.

On the other hand, if you picked *A student* as your option, you would be required to provide the name of the institution you attend, your field of interest, the zip code of your location, and country.

Please note that the zip code of your location is always a private information. So, even though the system displays your region, it keeps your zip code as private.

As you can see, the whole process is simple. Meanwhile, there is an opportunity to go for LinkedIn Premium account. Here, you would be requested to provide your street address in addition to the ones requested above.

Please, go over the details you provided again for the sake of accuracy. And to prevent issues in the future. Remember, LinkedIn is basically a platform for professionals and businesses.

Once you get to the end of filling required information based on the option you selected under this step, you can proceed to click *Continue*.

Step 3

Under this step, you are required to connect your email so as to import contacts from your phone book. While the two steps above are mandatory, this step is at your own discretion. But then, before you choose the side you want to stand, remember what we said about building a professional and standard profile?

Why should you take this option? It helps you grow your network easily. So, once you connect, you will be able to go through your address book to connect with or invite any email that is connected to a LinkedIn profile.

Some of the emails allowed for LinkedIn are Gmail, Yahoo mail, Gmail, Hotmail and others which didn't pop-up in the lists provided by the system.

Please note that whatever option you choose, you can't access your address book except you log in to your email account.

Also, be aware that not every email would match that of every person you think would be on LinkedIn. This is because some users created their LinkedIn account with a different email address.

Don't forget that this step is optional, so you can skip it if you so desire.

After you must have accepted or skipped the email address import option, a confirmation screen would appear telling you to confirm your email address in your email box.

The confirmation mail might deliver immediately or it might take a few minutes. Whichever way, you should take your time to confirm the message, enter your log-in details to access your LinkedIn profile. Once you are on your profile, begin to connect to professionals.

Can we now proceed to how you can create a company page or account?

How Do You Create A LinkedIn Company Account?

Having a LinkedIn company account is vital to a company's marketing strategy. Refer to chapter one where we talked about the benefits of a LinkedIn account to businesses. You can't just overlook them.

But before you rush into logging on to the website to register your business, make sure you have the right to carry out the LinkedIn page creation. And also, get your logo ready. The size of the logo that's advisable is 300 x 300pixel and make sure it's a square logo.

Before you go over the steps involved below, you should be reminded that having a LinkedIn profile is a requirement for creating a company.

Step 1

Creating LinkedIn company page is simple and straightforward as long as you look in the right direction.

To create a page, you should navigate to the top right corner of the page where you will find a tab labelled "Work".

Once you click, a list will drop down for you to pick "Create a Company Page". This is at the bottom. Find the (+) sign, then click on it.

Whether you are a Premium member or not, having a standard personal account is important to setting up a page for your company. Premium member or not, a personal account is important to setting up a company page. However, if you just have to create a new account for this purpose, you would have to wait for some weeks to be able to create a company page.

Step 2

At this stage, you will be required to supply all necessary data for your business page. The first piece of information which you would supply is the name of the business.

Pay careful attention to the title case, make sure you input the same way you want LinkedIn to show your name.

In the second box, you would be required to add the business URL. This is not complicated at all. The name of your business would have been added automatically to the second box with a dash in between the texts that make the company name. It's okay if you want take out the dashes to make it straightforward and functionally related with your brand. Or you could just opt for a URL that is the similar to what obtains on social sites like Facebook. Take a company called Building Nations Initiative for example, the URL will automatically appear as linkedin.com/company/building-nations-initiative.

And on your own, you could edit it to reappear as linkedin.com/company/buildingnationsinitiative.

After doing that, you should proceed to provide a means of verification to show that you have the official right to do so.

Also available is the option to create a University page. The features available include a section for alumni. You should contact LinkedIn if you plan to set up this kind of page.

Step 3

Here, you have to take your time to work on setting the outlook of the page to align with the company. What is being referred to is the branding your page. And you can't afford to neglect this.

To begin with, you should set up the page's cover image. Why is this necessary? The display of cover images are not usually the same depending on whether you logged in on a desktop or mobile browser. Now, you should go for size 1536 x 768 – this is the perfect size. And don't forget to design a cover image that grabs the entirety of what your business represents.

And a quick tip for the wise: Resist the temptation to use a cover that has text or word.

Once you are done with setting the cover image, uploading your business logo is the next. Remember we advised that you get the logo ready before you even start the page creation.

It is not advised that you use a personal profile, like the photo of your company's CEO, while you prepare the logo. After all, you are dealing with professionals and businesses on a professional platform.

Step 4

Next, you should provide LinkedIn with a detailed description of your company and what it does. Don't forget that whatever you say here is going to be the first point of contact which any prospective client on that platform would have. So, don't neglect the need to put in your best.

Of course, you should have between 1500 – 2000 words description for this. But sometimes, that's not enough. Even if it's just a 1000 words description, make sure it's relevant and compelling. Don't forget to use the right SEO keywords too. More often, it's about the in-depth quality description and not the length.

To make creating your description easier, outline the objectives which your business wants to achieve through the page. Map out your target audience from the crowd of professionals and businesses on LinkedIn, identify the unique selling point of your company, note the benefits your company; and more importantly, declare how these benefits improve the lives of your target.

Creating relevant and quality description requires perspective. And you don't need to rush the steps. Relax. And take your time to do this.

And don't just write and post. Do a self-edit, and hire a proofreader to go through it if your company does not have one.

After that, pick the areas of special interest of your business. Pick as much as you can for your business – there are about 20 special areas of interest. But be authentic. Make sure that whatever area of specialty you pick, your company really has it. The social space is full of fake claims already, don't increase the number.

Step 5

Under this step, all you have to do is include important details which are the type and size of your company, the year it was founded, website address, industry/field, and location.

If your company has locations distributed across a region or territory, you should pick one main office – the head office.

Step 6

This step gives you the opportunity to add groups to your business page. The pages you can add could be the one you own or those you are sure would contribute positively to the growth of your target and ultimately, your page.

Step 7

These are options you can return to attend to after publishing your page. This step allows you to include tagline, call to actions (CTAs), among others.

For your CTAs, you can incorporate the any of these – *learn more, contact/call us now, visit our website, register here, sign up, we can chat,* among others.

You can make the most of the call to action feature by inputting a URL that can ease the process of directing users to a conversion funnel on your website.

Step 8: Content Creation

You don't need to be told that for your business to thrive, you have to embrace content marketing. Meanwhile, don't get it all wrong. Content goes beyond text format. It encompasses images, short videos, infographics, and others.

You should note that the extent of your company's growth has a lot to do with your level of consistency with uploading content. The growth of the company page depends on the frequency of your content marketing.

To ensure consistent content marketing, you could use software for scheduling your activities.

LinkedIn Premium Account

This is a paid plan which you can pick if you are ready to upgrade your free version LinkedIn account. And this comes with massive features. So, you can assume that it would be worth the price and effort. Should you decide to upgrade, you get to enjoy a month-free trial.

Once the free-trial expires, you start to pay for subscription. The payment plan available are monthly and annually. You should the one you think you are fine with.

Some of the features available under this package are:

- Unrestricted open/direct messages.
- Access to premium content.
- Premium search filters.
- Great search functionality.
- Open membership link.
- Opportunity to view your profile viewers.
- Response to questions in a business day.
- LinkedIn badge.
- Unique and improved communications system, and others.

Now, based on your field of interest, there are four accounts that you can select pick from for your upgrade. They are:

- Recruiter Lite
- Job Seeker
- Business Plus
- Sales Navigator

Recruiter Lite:

This premium upgrade attracts a monthly fee. And it is specifically for businesses who are in search of new talents for recruitment.

The user interface design of Recruiter Lite package was designed with an intent – simplification of staffing process.

The features are slot management, targeted search, InMail management, profile management, reporting and analytics, and other collaborative tools.

Also, LinkedIn Recruiter Lite grants unrestricted access to 30 InMail messages every month for each member of the team. What's more? The InMail feature lets each member interact directly with professionals.

With this package, there is unrestricted access to unlimited profiles with suggested ones.

There are many more. And you can bet that LinkedIn won't stop at these. The journey towards simplifying recruitment process has just started.

Job Seeker:

Are you a job seeker? Do you know anyone seeking job opportunities? This package is for job seekers. While the prerequisite for use may not be the same, operating it demands a monthly fee in order to use certain features.

Some of the features are option to show your badge indicating that you are a job seeker on your profile. Also, you have the opportunity to access those who viewed your profile in 90 days. This is one of those features which distinguishes a free account from a premium. And should you find recruiters that interest you, you have the chance to message them directly. The InMail feature grants you 5 for every month and this comes with a guaranteed credit return if no InMail response comes in seven days.

Business Plus:

It's not enough to be a professional. Life becomes easier when you are able to connect with like-minds. To make this possible, Business Plus package brings this amazing solution to everyone. With a monthly fee, you get introduced to 25 profiles, about 3rd degree suggestions, and you can carry out additional search yourself to help you boost your network.

In addition, you get 15 InMails monthly alongside 7days response guarantee. Plus, you have up to 30 email credits – unused ones will roll over into another month.

What's more? This upgrade allows you to compare your performance with your connections. This is possible because you get to see a monthly overview of your performance.

Sales Navigator:

This upgrade is an integration with the technology from Point Drive that allows you to improve your sales target. With insights derived from the huge database that's available, this gives you an unrestricted chance to connect with prospects that need your services.

This is recommended for the sales representative of any company. With this tool, you get to evaluate and monitor the conversations of your targets while leading them carefully to your platform offline and then into a purchase channel.

LinkedIn also uses your history to recommend leads for your business using this tool. Again, this upgrade allows you to get updates concerning high-ranking decision makers working with contacts in your list. You shouldn't take this for granted if you care about ascertaining the type of users you are communicating with. Or don't you want to be abreast of actions like content shares, company and general contact updates of the contacts on your list?

Based on the analysis above, you shouldn't forget that whatever premium service you select need to align with your need as an individual, professional, or business. It is recommended that you take your time to grab the way the premium features operate, that's why LinkedIn offers 1 MONTH FREE TRIAL.

How To Make Payment For Premium Account

Before you can make payment, you will be required to provide your LinkedIn password for verification. After this, you have to pick a payment option of your choice. You have an option between PayPal account and Credit Card. The option you choose will determine the details you would be required to submit next.

A payment receipt would be sent to your email address alongside a printable one on your screen. If you want to close the on-screen receipt, you should click on the button which reads "I'm done".

Following that, you will be directed to click the "Start your free trial button". This is made available so as to let you get to understand how the plan you must have selected works.

This means that you can cancel if you end up not liking your choice. In order not to get billed, make sure you cancel the plan before the one month free trial expires.

Chapter 3:
How to Create a LinkedIn Profile That Sells

As mentioned earlier, your LinkedIn profile is the first chance you have to create a lasting impression on any prospect who comes across your profile. Don't take the need to have a standard profile for granted. In fact, as a marketer, it's not your after-thought at all. Put in all the effort you have at your disposal into creating one. You don't need to rush over doing this. This is after all, the first chance you have to say something unique and impacting about your brand.

Don't just say, show your prospects through the carefully selected words on your page that you understand what they are going through and that you have the needed solution. So, whatever you have to say on your profile must be detailed enough to lead the prospect to buy your product or service.

To sell and be successful as a business, you need to build a good profile on your LinkedIn account. You have the best platform to build a strong network, it's yours to take.

Thus, this chapter will take you through how you can optimize your LinkedIn account and profile to do the following:

- Have a strong network for your business or brand.
- To gain trust that leads to conversion.
- And eventually make sales.

Vital Characteristics of a LinkedIn profile

A LinkedIn profile needs to have the following characteristics if it must achieve its goal as a viable sales channel. These characteristics are considered below:

- A clear display picture –headshot with a good background, on your profile. And make sure it's a recent one. Have a smile on your face too, you are trying to attract, remember?
- A background banner that clearly represents your brand or where you work.
- A headline that is not only compelling but also of high-quality. Your headline should summarize the service you offer in simple and clear terms.
- Additional media like video, audio, infographics, graphs, and so on that accent how you intend to help your prospects.

- Lastly, you need to create a profile summary that extends the narrative of how you may be of help to your prospective buyers.

Does A Good Profile Influence Sales?

There is no magic to boosting sales, all you can find is marketing strategies that you can incorporate to get there. And while being on LinkedIn is one of those strategies, having a good profile on your account is an added advantage.

In fact, by now, you should have discovered that there are various features that LinkedIn allows you to take advantage of if your business and brand want to survive in this age of social media evolution.

The means by which you can appeal to prospects are large, and having a good profile is the first point of contact. So, yes, a GOOD profile influences sales.

Note the emphasis on good. This is more about how you create your profile using the right content with a cue about how your targets make informed buying decision and the kind of keywords they input in the search engine as they progress from the first step on the sales funnel to the last.

With your profile, you can either establish yourself as someone they need to go through to meet their needs or they can go ahead to seek help elsewhere.

In the chapters to follow, we will go through how the type of so influences the decision to start a conversation with you or not. You just need to do this right with carefulness. Just so you know. We will talk about this in depth later.

So, what do you do to have the right profile that brings you useful connections and followers? Pay attention to the following. Are you ready?

Build Your Profile Through The Eyes of the Buyers

You don't just jump into creating a profile because LinkedIn requires you to create a profile. As a marketer, you even need to be more intentional here. Don't just talk about your career achievements, where is the place of your targets? The question your target are going to be asking is beyond what your qualifications are. The question is: What are you offering us owing to your career achievements?

To win, you have to shift the narrative on your profile. Be more buyer-focused. What you should flaunt is your capacity to provide the solutions that they need. They want a better life, they want to grow and improve their standards; that's why they are on your profile in the first place.

If your content fails to show them these, be sure that they will move on.

Okay, its fine to talk about your achievements, but don't let that be the ultimate. Show, don't just tell, how you intend to add positively to their lives, businesses, among others. Your LinkedIn profile should show your prospective customers how you intend to help them. How resourceful are you about eliminating their challenges? And to them, your answer is all that matters.

Incorporate a Stunning Headshot Photo

As mentioned earlier, having the right profile picture is part of the deal. And it must be a professional shot. This is not one of those pictures you take with your phone. Plus, it must be recent. We are emphasizing recent because it must align with what you really look like should any of your connection decide to have a physical meeting with you.

We advise against using a logo as your profile photo because this is about you as a brand rather than a company. Besides, doing so is against LinkedIn's user's agreement.

Meanwhile, you have no excuse for leaving your profile photo box empty. You are on a social media platform for professionals, most of them would be interested in seeing the image of who they are dealing with. Besides, if you want to enjoy a 40% chance of getting quick responses to your InMail, and having more profile views, you should have a professional profile picture.

Note the following professional profile photo tips for LinkedIn and any other:

- Smile warmly with minimal exposure of your teeth.
- Keep your eyes on the camera.
- The photo should only go from your head to shoulders.
- Go with head-waist frame if need be.
- Don't use sunglasses.
- Use a white background, avoid colored clothing.

And don't forget to use background banner. It helps you draw attention to your brand early enough. If you have a company you work with, incorporate the colors and logo of the brand into your header to make it whole.

Create a Great Headline

Like in news reporting, the headline is important to attracting viewers to your profile. So, here, how you headline your profile matters. Not only must it be catchy, simple, and rich, it must be compelling. While this seems like what anyone could create without stress, after all, it's just not more than 120 characters or lower; you need to do it carefully.

Among other things, it should encourage them to want to know more about you, the service you provide, and how you can solve their problems.

By now, you should understand that your headline is not something you create in a rush as well. Take your time, identify the right keywords to use based on your market niche, and incorporate the kind of words that your targets can identify with even when carrying out a search.

In order to win with the right headline, you should use the right keywords, include the name of your company, and include how you can be of help to your prospects.

Are you wondering how you are supposed to do these within a 120 characters limit? It's possible, don't you think?

What about saying, for example:

An Account Integrator that Helps Bank Users in America to Analyze Transactions and Eliminate Wasteful Subscriptions/Emma Inc.

What has the headline above done?

- It stated who the targets are.
- It also stated what the company does.
- It identified the geographical location.
- It identified the problem. And since targets want solutions to bank overdraft fees and other wasteful hidden charges, they would definitely interested to look further into a profile with that kind of headline.

Can you do more than that in 120 characters? Yes.

Make Your Profile Summary Compelling

Yes, you need to use this 2000 characters currency you have to make a compelling profile summary. In details, let your targets know your engagement, the company you work for, and then, who you are. Don't forget to make this appear to be about your audience – the benefits you bring to them, if you want to drive increased conversion rate.

SEO is highly important here. Use the right keywords to drive home the needs of your prospects. Show them, through your profile summary that you are an indispensable resource to sending away their problems. That means you have to be compelling. Using the right keywords help your profile summary to rank top in search results each time a prospect launches a search query.

Your Use of English is a Criteria

In all you do, don't forget that you are on a social media platform for professionals who pay serious attention to details. While you are there to attract prospects, you shouldn't take your use of English for granted. What we are trying to say is that you must respect the rules of grammar. This includes tenses, punctuations, spellings, and others.

You never can tell how a single error could turn a big prospect off. You never can! So, it's best not to be careless. Put the right time into checking and re-checking every of your content. Hire a professional content editor even after you must have done your self-editing.

No matter how great the content looks to you, don't be in a hurry to update it. Don't be too lazy to go over any content over and over again. If you must make a good impression on your profile, you can't be too careless with details.

Everything matters, don't forget this.

Meanwhile, you should write with purpose. What do you want them to see through your profile summary? If they can't see that you can represent yourself in a good light, how do you expect them to trust you with representing them well?

How you write and use language –buyer centered, will either make them stay or go to another profile. Ultimately, the goal is to convince them enough to make them take action. If the message you intend to pass across is heavy with grammatical errors, you don't expect that they would be willing to take actions. Do you?

Include Media

To make your profile whole, including media is the way to go. Besides, this will further mold your credibility and help you gain trust. With the URL, you can upload video, presentation, and visuals related to your business.

This is part of you showing them how you can solve their problems. The media you upload could be about your previous projects for a client. And where a picture speaks louder than a thousand words, you can imagine how much more a video would do?

You can always upload media to your profile summary or on the Experience section.

Optimize the Experience Section

Here is your chance to tell your prospects about yourself and what you are engage in. With 2000 characters freedom to express, make sure you highlight your attributes, services, and USPs.

Below is a list of how you should manage your Experience section:

- What you do as well as who you are.
- Previous job experiences and the roles you played in customer satisfaction.
- Include link to media that's related to what you do/who you are.

You should know there are quite a number of LinkedIn account pushing for the same thing, so do it well. To be taken more professionally, you should link the LinkedIn page of your company. With this, the logo of your company would be on display mode and this goes a long way to give you a more strategic positioning.

Understand Your Company's Policies

Never take any online action that goes against the in-house policy of your company. So, before you add any employer under your current job description, be sure it's okay to do so.

Check and re-check any claim you are making about any employer or position. It's important to build a complaint-free LinkedIn profile if you want to gain the attraction of prospective buyers.

Leave no Field Untouched

For a professional social media site like LinkedIn, nothing can take the place of having a fully-completed profile. Ensure you leave no field untouched – that's the best recommendation anyone can give you. Why is this important? Prospective buyers are more eager to pay attention to a marketer whose profile is complete than the one who is not. Do you understand that?

So, take your time to talk about your educational history; you have 2000 characters to do this. Talk about how the moments spent in school shaped you.

Add your skills, and don't forget the need to continually update them. There is always room for growth, isn't it? While you can include as many skills as you want, make sure to stick to the relevant to you.

What's more? More like the likes that you get on Facebook from friends and contact for your activities, you can give your endorsements to people you know after highlighting your skills. Meanwhile, you can only do this after you must have turned on the endorse feature in your setting.

Recommendation is another area on your profile creation that brings you a lot of positive effects. First, be willing to write heart-felt recommendation for those you have met and worked with in your career path. It's even possible that you are still working with them. At the same time, don't hesitate to seek the recommendation of those who have worked with you too. Just make sure their recommendations align with skills you have indicated on your profile.

- Why should you give and seek recommendations?

Search engines are likely to index your recommendation segment when people carry out search queries about what you do. If the right keywords have been used in this segment, this is an added advantage that helps you appear top in search results pages.

Every successful marketer on LinkedIn understands this to be a vital tool that can help bring the kind of leads with a promising rate of conversion.

Standard Profile Is Important to the Success of Your Sales

Once again, as a marketer, having a standard profile on LinkedIn is significant to your success. If you have been failing at selling on LinkedIn, it's time to go and re-evaluate your profile. Don't get wrong though. We are not saying that's the solution, it's just the best place to begin at if you want to change the narrative.

Most times, the success you experience as a marketer who gets the attention of the market begins with your profile.

Chapter 4:
Determining Your Ideal Customers

Having established the tips for creating a customer-focused profile, we can bet that you already know how this goes a long way to boost your conversion rate.

So, it's time to talk about how to determine the ideal customers for your business. We understand that for most marketers, the problem is not usually about creating a client-focused profile, but determining who an ideal customer is.

Please, although we talked about connecting with those you know by using a feature that allows you to link your contact list to your LinkedIn account, you should know that there will always be an exception.

Here is the warning: When it comes to determining the ideal customer for your business, your families and friends don't always have a place. In fact, they are usually the one who have little or no interest in the product or service you offer.

You need to stop making assumption as a marketer. Don't put your marketing hopes in the same basket with your families and friends so as not to be disappointed. So, how do you ascertain the ideal customers for your products and services?

This chapter offers unique strategies that can help you identify your ideal customers. Are you ready?

Create A Profile of Your Ideal Client

There is no other way to it than first creating a profile that you would attract an ideal customer. And while we have talked, in the preceding chapter about how to create a standard profile, you still need to need to do a self-assessment using the questions set below. The answers you are able to give to these questions will help you determine your ideal customer.

- What category of users usually have the problem my product or service solves?

- What type of user would be ready to pay for my products and services at the set fee?

You need to find the answers to these questions because while you may have the product or service that solves the problems of everyone, not everyone would be interested in buying. Besides, not everyone would be ready and able to pay the price you have set on your products or services. With the answers to the questions above already determined, you should now examine the following:

- In what region or country do my ideal customers live? Consider their city and time-zone.
- What age-bracket do my ideal customers belong?
- Would you rather target individuals, groups, or companies?
- And lastly, what's the gender of my ideal customers?

Have it at the back of your mind that you can't have everyone in the market to yourself. Almost everyone is already taking, all you have to do is take a part. That's why it's important to identify your ideal customers.

So, what's next?

Add them together

At this point, you should add your product or service offered with the profile that's focused on your ideal customer. Once again, include adequate details.

Let's assume that you have found out that the work time in the city of your ideal customers is 12.00pm – 3.00am EST, you can set your line like this:

Ryan is a brand expert in xxxxx and can only offer services to customers from 12.00pm – 3.00am EST.

Please, there is no point in rushing anywhere. There is no plan to shut down LinkedIn, neither are your targets going anywhere. Whether they found you first or you did, the roads that leads there is a standard profile that's customer-centered.

Identify Your Collaborators – Companies or Individuals

After discovering your ideal customers and using them as guide to create your profile, the next thing is to search for the individuals or companies you would love to collaborate with. Use the search tool on Google to find prospective collaborators, then you can connect with the ones suitable for your business on LinkedIn.

How Do You Establish Connection?

Once again, not business an ideal customer as far as B2B marketing is concerned. So, you need to first identify the point of connection you have in respect to interest. Is it a first, second, or third degree connection? Do you have any personal relationship?

If there is a personal relationship, you should consider getting to know them via LinkedIn or a call. Don't just ask about family and old friends and end it there. This should be a means to requesting for an introduction to the top decision maker in his/her organization, so do it well like the professional you are.

If there is no one you have a close bound to introduce you to the individual or company, you can scan through the LinkedIn followers of the company. Be assured that there will be two or more employees of the company also following the company's updates. Evaluate them, pick a viable employee that can lead you to the company and connect with him or her.

Identify Ideal Customers Using Area(s) of Shared Interest

In as much as we are unique individuals, we usually have people with whom we share interest. And as a marketer, this is worth tapping into. Isn't this the reason seasoned salespersons have consistently advised that we market only what we believe in? Verily, when you find a target who shares your belief, it becomes easier to convert them.

Meanwhile, it doesn't have to be entirely or directly an interest in the product or service you sell. The common ground could be working in an industry similar to yours or a company that requires your product or service.

It could also be the grad school which you both attended or a mutual friend or group membership on some virtual or physical space.

No matter how small the shared interest it, find a way around it.

Path to Successfully Marketing to Your Ideal Clients

The journey has just started after identifying your ideal client and connecting with them on LinkedIn.

Don't just throw what you sell in their face, it's a path you need to thread with care. So, what are the marketing strategies you can take on LinkedIn?

- Post articles consistently.
- Add resourceful images, videos, webinars, and so on.
- Comment, like, and share what they do as well.

- Don't forget to respond to their comments on yours.
- Make sure whatever you do is relevant to your market niche and useful to them.

When you do the above with dedication and consistency, it wouldn't be long to gain their trust and loyalty. Eventually, they will be interested in what you are marketing when the time comes.

How Do You Find Your Niche on LinkedIn?

While LinkedIn might have been created with professionals in mind, it doesn't mean it's strictly for professionals. Based on this wrong notion, a lot of marketers do miss out on many opportunities that LinkedIn offers.

In fact, individuals and many more are yet to join this amazing platform for the same reason. And we can't blame them. LinkedIn focuses more on B2B networking.

But, in addition, it is also a resourceful platform for individuals in various market niche. And it's not complicated to find your way around networking like it's assumed by those who have failed to sign up.

Now, let's discuss how you can identify your niche and tips for establishing connections with those in it.

How to Identify Your Niche On LinkedIn

Follow Thought-leaders in Your Industry

From the beginning, LinkedIn launched an RSS reader called *LinkedIn Today*. The aim of this was to pile content across the whole users on the platform and only to share the one relevant to your market niche with you.

Later, in 2013, *LinkedIn Pulse* -a feed app was launched. So, you have an opportunity to customize your newsfeed by yourself. To do this, you can use the following metrics:

- Channels
- •Authors
- Influencers

It's possible that you will find your market niche in all of the categories above. However, the best place to look is with the influencers. This is because when you set it to influencers in your niche, it is possible to get access to unlimited subjects as long as they are labelled under your niche.

What's more? You will find like-minds who are also doing the same thing – identifying with influencers in your market niche, to network with and eventually market to.

Use Targeted Keywords to Discover Specific Niche-Relevant Groups

You can connect with members of your market niche via groups, tribes, and communities. They are easy to find – input relevant keywords into the search bar offered by LinkedIn. When the results pop-up, you still the choice to scan through. Once you found the one that meets your niche, send membership request immediately.

Once again, don't try to throw what you sell in their face as soon as you join if you are a marketer. And don't be in a haste to start posting content. Learn. Understand how the in-house policy works. But that's not a reason to be inactive. While waiting and learning, do the following:

- Comment.
- Ask question.
- Seek clarifications where you don't understand what the writer or admin is trying to say.

And do it all professionally. It's easier to like and move on that's why it's not on the bullet list above. You need to do more than like, comment.

Try Direct Connections

It's okay if you don't want to go through the steps above. You can take the direct path by sending direct connection request to the targets in your market niche. Remember we talked about this earlier?

On the other hand, you could use *the people you may know* feature. This is a resource made available by LinkedIn and they cover persons who share a connection via other related contacts or belong to a group with you. At least, you don't have to explain to this people why you are sending a connection request.

Based on what we have covered so far, you would agree with us that LinkedIn is an ideal platform for connecting with your ideal customers. It offers viable win-win situation if only you would take your time to study what your ideal customer is likely to input in the search engine, the kind of content your ideal customer would be more interested in, the kind of aspiration that he or she fancies, among others.

It's a give-take situation as well. When you do it well, you are on your way to making connections that lead to conversion in the end.

Are you ready for the next chapter?

Chapter 5:
Best LinkedIn practices

LinkedIn is a massive social media site for professionals and individuals with career perspective. Unlike Facebook, Instagram, and other social media platforms that connect you to all sort of people, LinkedIn uses a direction.

How? This is an algorithmically driven process in which, based on your profile, you are connected to people who share the same perspective with you.

What's the implication of this? It means you have to follow the best practices encouraged by the platform in order to be strategically positioned. Whatever is your goal – to build a community of leads for your business, content marketing, job seeking, among others, it's important that you adhere to bet practices on LinkedIn.

LinkedIn cannot be scorned if you or your organization is interested in building a professional community. And to thrive on LinkedIn, adhering to best practices is a must. As a result, this chapter talks about some of the best practices you should embrace alongside the mistakes that should be avoided.

Are LinkedIn Best Practices Necessary?

According to *About LinkedIn, 2019*, there are about 3 million business pages on LinkedIn. Thus, there is no mistaken, joining this social medium is one of the best things that could happen to any business. Yes, if you want your business to grow and develop.

Whatever meaningful result you look forward to achieving for your business, refer to the benefits of LinkedIn in Chapter one, it's possible on LinkedIn.

However, to enable effective growth, you need to adhere to LinkedIn best practices because they are necessary.

Thus, you should take your time to understand the practices discussed below. They are pivotal to you, your organization, and its brand.

Determine Your Type of Content

Content is king. So, if you are not creating and posting content on LinkedIn, you should start now. As a business, content is an effective marketing strategy that is aimed at your targeted customers – to drive them from the stage of awareness on the sales funnel to the point where they buy.

And when it comes to posting content on LinkedIn, there are many provisions that you should be aware of. Examined below are a number of effective content that you can run on LinkedIn.

Clickable Content: There are about 3 million users on LinkedIn, some of them are connects based on your profile. If you are interested in drawing their attention to your LinkedIn profile, you need to post content consistently. But is that automatic? No. We can bet that there would be a number of them who would just walk over your content probably because your content doesn't compel them to lean in and look.

The point then is that your content needs to be compelling and engaging. You can't afford to be bland and uninteresting when it comes to content creation on LinkedIn. Your connections have a lot on their feeds already, whether you will be given attention or not depends on how you present what you are trying to say.

Can your content push your readers to want to know more in the next page? That's the essence of a clickable content.

One of the content marketing strategies that makes this possible is visual. Numbers from research indicated that visual content are the major drivers on LinkedIn. So, if your content contains images, animations, infographics, and many more, users are more likely to click.

What are we saying in summary? Avoid plain text. Black and white is no longer enough.

Another tip is to include a call-to-action (CTA). Every reader has a behavior which you are trying to modify and at the point in your content marketing, you shouldn't miss the chance to make them take an action. That's what CTA is about. If you don't tell them to click for more or start a free trial, they are not likely to think so themselves.

Identify Specific Audience: Being specific about audience is one of the LinkedIn best practices that you should embrace. As we have told you earlier, everyone is not your target. So, as long as you have a market niche, you need to know those who belong to you and those who are not.

Within this same frame, you need to create content that will appeal to your specific audience. To gain the insight that can help you channel your content to the right persons, you need to evaluate using the following criteria:

- Who reads my content? Those who view and then you read your content are your target audience. Face those who clicked through and direct your content to them. Meanwhile, we are not saying you should neglect the possibility of gaining the attention of others. Our emphasis here is the need to know who/what your priorities are.

- Who are my LinkedIn followers? It takes someone who is interested in your profile to follow you. So, study your followers. This is how you identify your major demographic group.

- Who do I target? Content is a marketing strategy to help you identify those you should target among the crowd. Identify those you can target and work towards creating the right content for them.

Stimulate Interests: Posting content on LinkedIn because everyone is doing so won't lead you or your business anywhere. You just have to be strategic with your effort. The moment you identify your targets, you should apply methods to your content creation strategy. So, apart from using visuals, you should not fail at stimulating their interest. How do you do this?

- Post content that give them insight about the industry they belong to.

- Discuss topics relevant to them.

- Ask questions always. Make sure that the questions are those that would prompt the, to want to find out more.

- Be engaging. High-level of engagement is part of your CTA. Require them to share similar experience in the comment section, ask them to give your suggestions, and so on.

Promote Industry-related Events: As the largest social media network, there would always be crowd-pulling industry-related events making round. And for you, it makes good sense to talk about them. Meanwhile, don't just post and re-share, build conversations around them.

While you are promoting the cause of the event, you could do little exposition on the topic by asking prospective participants what they look forward to learning. It's a way by which you can pique their curiosity. You could do this on your LinkedIn account or on the group created for would-be participants.

In terms of content marketing, you could create content around the event. To do this effectively, the event needs to be related to your brand coverage.

Visual Appeal: As emphasized in preceding chapter, adding media files is very resourceful. This means that even your font color must be engaging. Don't turn-off your targets with boring images, make sure any image you use accents the point you are trying to say in the next. You don't have to have a sophisticated graphic designing skill neither do you have to necessarily hire the service of one. There are free working graphic tools like ***Canva*** and *Piktochart* that you can use to create related images. All-in-all, make sure that your infographic is highly practical and in-depth.

Career-Focused: Remember we mentioned that creating relevant content for your audience is all you should do first. No business should rush into throwing promotional pieces in the face of their targets. Except you create value first, don't sell. Of course, we all know that a marketer has to sell. But to pays to show your targets that you care about them beyond what you are selling.

One of the ways to do this is through update of career-focused content. Doing this within the frame of the industry you share with them will not only establish you as a thought-leader, but also as someone they could trust.

So, in your content, talk about how things work in respect to leadership, management, promotion, team-bonding, and add links to open positions, if available.

Encourage Your Staff Members to Post Brand-Content

The employees of any business or organization are its primary brand's image makers. Consequently, it's expected that a business would optimize this. How do you optimize this?

- Make sure they join LinkedIn.

- Some of them would probably antagonize this move. So, don't force them to do so. All you should do is help them understand the benefit it brings to their own personal career growth. If need be, hire someone who is an expert on LinkedIn account management to guide them through. And then, encourage them to use their presence to promote the brand by posting brand-focused content on behalf of the company.

- You can provide them with content creation idea lists that speaks for your brand. This is being recommended it's possible that some of them wouldn't know what to post.

- Meanwhile, make sure they are kept abreast of the activities of the organization.

- And lastly, always treat them right. When your employees are satisfied, it becomes easier for them to talk about you on social media sites.

Optimize LinkedIn Pulse

Any business that wants to enjoy holistic reach, should key into LinkedIn Pulse. This feature enables publishing of relevant content. Unlike what you post on your LinkedIn profile, what are the benefits of LinkedIn Pulse?

- Improved and focused targeting since your content will reach does that it matters to and eventually, you get to evaluate the demographic factors of your targets.

- When your publication gets high social shares, you become a top ranking by Pulse. You can imagine what this means for your company or brand.

- With LinkedIn Pulse, you have a chance to create contents with backlinks. This brings you numerous SEO benefits.

- Like regular blog activities established by your business, you can tag content in your publication. What's the implication of this? Your searchability increases and you enjoy numerous benefits over and over again when you appear on SERPs.

- Content marketing is a strategy common to most businesses. At least, those online. This means that there are more than enough content for online users to deal with. As a result of this, content marketing is highly competitive. LinkedIn pulse is an opportunity to beat this competition.

Now, how do you beat the competition?

1. Create content that is within a thousand words limit.
2. Make sure it has a great headline.
3. Focus on industry/career subject matters.
4. Include media files such images, videos, animations, and infographics.
5. Avoid content that involve influencers.

Remain Active

Let's put it this way: our level of activeness influences your visibility online. So, you need to stay active. When you become inactive, you kill the interest of your followers. If you want to build trust and followership, you need to spend quality time on LinkedIn. Because we understand it is not easy creating content consistently throughout the day, you should do the following so as to stay relevant on LinkedIn.

- Post at least once in a day. If you can do more, fine. We recommend that you have your posting schedule before or after business hours.

- Be engaging. Like posts, pass comment if you have something reasonable to say, and we advise that you join groups.

- Continually update your skills, business details, cover photos, and others.

- Incorporate videos. If pictures could say more than a thousand words, how much more a video?

- Post job openings and scholarship opportunities.

- Let you readers and followers see you as human. Businesses having social media sites seems absurd but as long as you can be human, you will win. Be in conversations, be genuine, show love to your followers – wish them happy birthday, re-share their useful posts too, and so on.

Use LinkedIn Analytics to Track Your Success

Being able to measure your success on LinkedIn is good especially when you need to execute content marketing strategies that generate results. To gain insights concerning your efforts, the metrics highlighted below are necessary:

- **Visitor Demography:** Through this, you can discover who reads your content. Once you see their list, you can find their job description, industry, location, level, company's staff size, function, and so on.

- **Views:** Over a particular period of time, you get to see how many people viewed your company's page.

- **Impression:** This refers to the number of times your content was shown to LinkedIn users.

- **Click:** This refers to the numbers of time LinkedIn users clicked on the name of your company, the logo, title, or content.

- **Follower:** This lets you know the number of followers you gained from a sponsored post.

- **Engagement:** This describes the number of impressions which has been divided by the interactions which LinkedIn users have with your posts.

- **Audience:** Your audience describes those who viewed your post. You get to know whether it's viewed by every of your followers or just a particular segment.

Getting More Results Using LinkedIn

As a marketing expert, you will be expected to use all the LinkedIn resources at your disposal to make things work. There will be a lot for you to use. So, if your company is not on LinkedIn, now is the time. However, you should beware not to abuse the resources at your disposal. What are we saying? You should be human when using the tools made available to you.

For example, if you need to make sure your targets view your post, you should create contents that you would be willing to interact with yourself. And make sure whatever you post relates well with the focus and goal of your industry.

LinkedIn Mistakes That You Should Avoid

Once again, be reminded that About LinkedIn, 2019 reveals that there are about 610 million users on the platform. Also, there are about 10 million active job posts available on the platform.

Without doubt, this is the best professional social media site anyone with the intent of professional career growth could belong to.

But many of those who are active on other social media sites like Facebook, Instagram, and Twitter avoid LinkedIn because they think it's complicated. And they are right. On LinkedIn, a simple mistake or inattention could put a dent on your authenticity as a professional. Thus, you need to be careful about your activities on LinkedIn. So, what are the mistakes you should avoid on LinkedIn?

Not Creating Thorough Goals

As a marketer, don't neglect the need to have clearly stated goals on LinkedIn. Setting goals is your ultimate guide to optimizing your time on the platform and making sure whatever you do there is worth it.

In order to achieve your goals, you should spend quality time and effort on LinkedIn connecting with similar minds like you. However, don't be in a hurry. The fact that you have been told that LinkedIn helps your career and business, doesn't mean it's a magic.

You need to spend time building your profile as valuable. What can the headhunters who are searching for new talents take away from your profile? Does your profile them? Are your experiences and skills visible and valuable enough? Do you stand as someone who can help them solve the challenges of their business?

When you create a thorough goal for your LinkedIn profile, it becomes easier to get it right and achieve good result within a short period of time.

Your Profile Does Not Pronounce Your Expertise

Some LinkedIn users are on the platform to specifically headhunt for raw talents on behalf of their company. They are in the business of evaluating profiles. Thus, it's important that you set up your profile to pronounce exactly what you do.

There are features for setting up profiles to reflect the level of your expertise. The choice is yours to fill your profile up with the required details or not.

So, go back now to your LinkedIn account. Does it fully reflect your educational history, experience, and skills? Is it okay to even call your LinkedIn profile a virtual resume? Yes.

Don't be careless or lazy, it's easier to be judged by your poor grammar and punctuation in black and white. After all, it is expected that you should have taken your time to check and re-check.

Find quick tips below:

- Have a catchy headline.

- Create compelling profile summary.
- Post content relevant to your brand and industry.
- Consistently make it clear that you are a professional in your field.

You Share Too Personal Events

Although LinkedIn is also a social media site, it's designed with intent for professionals. Thus, you should be careful not post things that are deemed too personal. Unlike Facebook or Instagram, you can't show off your new car or upload a video of you taking your dog for a walk.

When it comes to content creation, you should be careful not to share wrong opinions or unfounded claims. These actions are so unprofessional. LinkedIn is not your private diary where you write secrets neither is it a playground where you talk lousily without care.

Whether on your wall or in groups, you should avoid arguments that lack intellectual base, avoid name-calling, among others. Keep complaints to yourself, you are probably not going to agree to everything that's shared on LinkedIn; and it's okay. Just be tolerant. If you can't show tolerance in a virtual space, how do you convince your would-be employee that the case would different when you finally get recruited by their company?

Anything that could turn away headhunters when found should be resisted.

Not Improving Your LinkedIn

Imagine a scenario where you finally get the job you have been looking for via LinkedIn. Before you got the job, you consistently follow the tips recommended in the previous chapters. And then, you got the job and the chapter to being visible on LinkedIn was closed. This is a great mistake that you should avoid.

One thing is true: You are not going to be on the job forever. Whether as a result of job dissatisfaction or the thirst for a career growth, you might have to eventually leave your present job. So, where do you return to when you need to raise your ladder? You return to LinkedIn again, right?

The message is that you should never neglect your LinkedIn account. Keep it updated with the right content. Stay relevant in your chosen industry. Learn new skills, get new certification, and update them on your profile. When you constantly update your profile, you become strategically placed when opportunities better than the one you have eventually appear.

Don't wait till you are searching for such opportunities before you start updating.

There is a warning though. Don't post too much. Always, the quality of content surpasses the quantity.

Neglecting Your Network

There is no point in following all the strategies for optimizing LinkedIn that we have given you and growing the right connections only for you to eventually neglect them.

You need to remain active. Even though we have advised you against posting too much, you should optimize your presence by joining industry-related groups. Once you are able to amass industry-related connections, you should manage what you have got so as to boost your legitimacy and genuineness.

Mind you, don't be too quick to send sales message or request for favors to your connections. Develop real relationships first.

Forgetting Keywords

Keywords are essential to optimizing your presence online. If you want to get found on LinkedIn, including keywords in your profile is second to none. When you have the keywords related to your industry in the right place – headline, job description, and profile summary, it will be easier to be found when headhunters use the search engine.

Let's assume that your marketing specialization is content writing, you should use keywords such as article, SEO content, and content marketing. These keywords help you to tank top in the search results made available by LinkedIn to the searcher.

Not Requesting for Help

You don't know it all and that's not a crime. It's only a crime if you fail to ask questions. As a newbie, you might end up neglecting the details that you ought to incorporate into your profile.

Thus, even when you are sure you have ticked all the sections, you should seek the help of a second eyes. We recommend that you seek the help of someone who understands how LinkedIn works. On a second note, the person can be someone in your industry who is also an expert LinkedIn user.

And don't be too personal when you creating your profile. You should thrive to leave a lasting impression on your profile viewers, so craft your story like it's about them and not you. So, rather than just talking about your educational history, highlight the skills that you have acquired. Highlight how these skills would help you serve the industry or company you are targeting, among others.

Chapter 6:
Creating the Content That Attracts on LinkedIn

Have you stopped to ask yourself the kind of content you would love to read if you were in your targets' shoes? We are requesting you to do this because it's more or less a fruitless effort if your content doesn't speak or resonate in the mind of your targets. Besides. What's the point if a content does not help you optimize your visibility?

As you evaluate your content marketing efforts so far, have it at the back of your mind that every content you publish on this professional social media site will go a long way to make or mar your brand building, whether personal or corporate.

In this chapter, we will take you through the strategies you can deploy in creating the right content. So, what are the types of content that you can optimize on your platform?

Blogs

The Ultimate List of Digital Marketing Statistics, 2019, reveals that over 80% of social media or modern marketers who use blog posts have a high return from their marketing investment.

So, as you can see, blogging is one of the ways by which your brand can reach many audience at a time. If you are planning to expand your network on LinkedIn and position your organization as an authority, blogging is a step in the right direction.

With LinkedIn publishing platform, you can post blog content rich in relevant information that consumers and businesses cannot turn their eyes away from.

Meanwhile, before you begin to blog you should create a goal for your blogging. Your goal could one or more of the following:

- Educating
- Informing, and
- Entertaining.

You can also incorporate entertainment into your blogs. Don't you know? But then, you should do this with the focus of your industry at the back of your mind. When it comes to educating and informing, you could write expert opinion and analysis or share the ones presented by authorities in your industry. Well, you don't have to be share directly. You can use link building to quote the authorities in your industry. Be reminded that link building is part of the strategies for ranking on SERPs. All you have to do is make sure it's relevant to what you are talking about in your blog post.

The types of blog content that you can share as blog via LinkedIn are:

- Opinion articles
- Guest writers
- Contribution of authorities to conversations.
- How-to content
- Flash stories
- Listicles
- Ultimate guides
- Newsworthy content

Images

Don't take for granted the importance of images. Not only are images cost-effective, they are also time-preserving.

But here is the warning – don't use pictures for the sake of doing so. Make sure whatever image you use resonates with your targets. Don't get it wrong though. Also, make sure it offers aesthetic value - that is, it must be visually appealing.

In addition, include catch descriptions and storyline around images especially if it's an image of your product. Even the image should be saved with the right keywords before you post online. Every description you ascribe to images should include the right keywords as well.

We understand that it is not that easy to create and post lengthy SEO content, so feel free to share thought-stimulating images on your LinkedIn page.

So, what are the types of images you can use on LinkedIn?

- Lifestyle images
- Pictures from industry-related images
- Products
- Cartoons

- Memes
- GIFs

Infographics

Never underestimate the power of infographics. In fact, infographics rank higher than blogs. With infographics, you can present research results to your targets, you can give illustrative examples, among others. It's a time-conversing way to keep your LinkedIn profile active if you don't have so much time at your disposal.

Like images and clear visuals, viewers are attracted to infographics. With infographics you get backlinks that you didn't even request for.

In addition, with infographics, it's easier to incorporate CTAs.

White Papers and Case Studies

White papers and case studies is a professional and corporate way to sell your brand. What is a white paper and a case study? White paper is a document which details research about your field or organization while case study is a more specific and in-depth research. In order words, while white paper is broad, case study is focused on a particular event.

What roles do these play in respect to your marketing strategy?

- White paper helps to showcase the strategic position of a company within the sector while emphasizing the expertise, creativity, reach, and history of the company.
- Case study showcases in clear terms the approach and methods used in initiating, negotiating, executing, and evaluating a project by a company in a given sector.

However, you shouldn't just incorporate these into your content marketing strategy because everyone else is doing so. Before you do, make sure whatever is contained therein is verified, proofread, and informative enough. Avoid irrelevant details that might rub a dent of unprofessionalism on your brand or company. Remember you are going to be presenting white papers and case studies most of the time in order to establish a connection with your targets, so do it well. At least, if it's worth doing.

Avoid bluffs. Abstain from boasting. And include only facts and necessary details. And don't forget to include the history of your company, the achievements, and level of clients' loyalty.

What more do you stand to gain from white papers and case studies?

- White papers and case studies contribute greatly to your blog site.

- They help you to attract old and new targets.
- They strengthen customers' loyalty.
- They generate viable leads.
- You can post them on your LinkedIn page with CTAs incorporated into them.

Video

Thanks to the revolution of digital age. With proper attention to detail, anyone can create video and share with their connections on LinkedIn. You can do this on your profile, page updates, or LinkedIn publisher.

Besides, according to Walters, 2015, about 75% of online traffic is earned by video updates alone.

Meanwhile, you don't just create video because everyone is doing it. If you must create video, you need to stand out. Ensure that your video has the right aesthetic, clear tones, useful idea, and high-level engagement.

Also, you should do your best to create educating, interesting, and informative video content if you are ready to do this. You don't want to create content that will put a dent on your brand. Not only must it represent the image of your brand well, it must adequately cater for the needs of your target audience.

It's an investment on your part, so don't waste your resources with no return.

Webinars

Webinars are participants to participants live events. Usually, it takes the form of interactive session between a brand and its viewers on a given platform. During the session participants can interact and also initiate chats.

According to Nguyen, 2015, study revealed that about 40% of webinar attendees usually turn into leads. Many business marketers are embracing webinar because it gives them the opportunity to put a face and human voice behind its brand and enjoy good feedback from targets.

If you haven't included webinar into your marketing tactics, now is the time to take your chance through LinkedIn by promoting your webinar and driving increased traffic to your website. On LinkedIn, a lot of individuals and professionals are eager to learn, so they sign up for webinars where they can interact with experts and professionals in their industry.

Podcasts and Audio

Podcast or audio is great resource which your business can use to build a strong LinkedIn network. If you intend to enjoy continued interaction and high level engagement, podcast or audio is ideal for you.

Gibbs, 2019, reveals that about 90% of podcast and audio subscribers are loyal to the brand whose content they hear.

So, the key is to create series of podcast and audio with mind-blowing content. It's important to supply them with quality content if you really want to build a community of dedicated followers. Give them what they love and they won't stop being dedicated to you.

Despite the tons of information that flood us daily, some digital users still miss out. So, you can channel your podcast or audio into keeping them informed about newsworthy event in your industry. Links to your podcast or audio can be put on your LinkedIn profile or attached to a visual.

Downloadables

Materials such as eBooks, ultimate guides, templates, report, and how- to, among others, which you give to your targets in exchange for their emails are what we refer to downloadables.

Downloadables are one of the ways to build an email list organically unlike having to buy one.

How do you get them to grant you're their email? Those ready to enjoy the content of your material, eBook for example, will be required to input their email in a box so that the material could be sent to them. Or, they could be required to create an account using their email address and password before they could download the content.

You can also share the link to any downloadable on your LinkedIn. Get ready to attract a massive traffic as well as generate leads if the content is relevant to your target audience.

Factors To Consider Before Choosing Your Type of Content

Apart from deciding on the type of channels to push your content through, it is important to know your brand and choose the type of content that's good for you.

Five factors need to be considered before choosing your type of content. They have been examined below:

- Know your goal: Creating content on LinkedIn is not something you jump into because everyone is doing it. You need to have a goal in order to give your content a direction. So, before you begin, ask yourself: What do I want to achieve with this content?

- Responsive Audience: Before you go ahead to create post, be sure about the kind of content that will stimulate response from your audience. You don't want to create content that your targets won't engage.

- Your Platform: No matter the number of followers and connections you have on any social platform, not all of them is fit for your content. You need to ascertain which among them will be receiving your content the most in the light of what your goal is.

- Social media: Will it be easy to post the content you create on social media platforms?

- Resources: It's not advisable to jump into content marketing because your competition is doing so. Even if you decided to, you don't have to do what they are doing. What you should ask yourself first is if you have the needed resources. By resources, we mean skills, money, and human capacity that would be required to consistently create quality posts, video, images, podcasts, and webinars, among others.

Above all, you shouldn't demotivate your targets or followers as a result of posting boring content. Spice it up, don't follow one way to doing it. Diversity is really important if you want to gain a wider audience with no barrier.

Effective use of Content Marketing

As a result of its structured approach to content marketing, most users prefer LinkedIn to Twitter. Thus, overtime, it has grown as the center of business-focused content promotion.

However, despite its increasing use, LinkedIn users still consider a certain question. The question is if indeed all content gains the same level of visibility?

Realistically, it's not always possible to get the desired level of visibility. But does that mean business marketers should forego their content marketing efforts? The answer is NO.

Remember we only said gaining the same level of visibility is not always possible. This means that marketers can become visible to their targets if they remain active on LinkedIn. We have earlier talked about the need to be active online as an individual, brand, or company.

Guide For LinkedIn Content Marketing Plan

The kind of content marketing you are doing depends on the platform you are aiming at. Above all else, creating the kind of platform that your targets can relate with is the most important.

Since LinkedIn is a platform created for stakeholders in industries, you need to create the kind of content that will help you gain their attention.

And there is no other way to it than creating the content that resonate with your audience to some professional degree. You are already aware that LinkedIn is the one of the platforms that give you industry results related to the goal of your business. Among other things, with the right content marketing strategy, you will gain loyal leads and boost the level of engagement you have.

Meanwhile, one virtue which you need to learn is being patient while waiting. It doesn't matter whether you know all the content marketing tips available, you need to be willing to let the progress take place without being in haste.

A lot of factors make LinkedIn different from other social media platforms. For example, you need endorsement from professionals who are authority in your industry for skills that you have included in your profile. Imagine if the managing director of an international financial institution endorses your skill as a financial advisor?

Owing to some of these striking differences, you need to have a content marketing strategy that meet the standard of B2B and B2C expected on LinkedIn. You have nothing to worry about though as there are content marketing tools that you can use to set yourself up for success. For example, showcase and company pages are the features that enable the creation of service leadership while InMail and related features facilitate the brand awareness activities of companies.

Like we have introduced you to some types of content earlier, you can boost the authority of your company through webinars, industry-related events, and eBooks, among others. And if you are interested in advertising, using sponsored posts feature is necessary.

More than anything, these features are useful for connecting with targets. Although the progress may only be measurable at a slow pace, you will always get results that are satisfactory.

To help you through this process, there are certain steps that your organization can follow. Some of the steps are considered below:

Focus on Your Network Growth

By now, you should have understood that LinkedIn is unique. Although it's a social media site, you should not forget that it's designed with an intent for professionals. So, your approach needs to differ.

Ordinarily, you can start by sending invitations to those who share the same interest with you. That's the most common method which anyone can use without stress.

Other simple methods include sending personalized message requesting for connection. To do this, make sure you:

- Have a detailed profile page.
- Be an active user on the groups you belong to.
- Attach your email signature to the LinkedIn URL.

Having been purchased by Microsoft, the website boasts of about 610 million users. What can you do with this number of users? You can create a large network for yourself among these users by publishing content on the platform, and doing so consistently.

Creation of Company Page

In a previous chapter, you learnt about how to set-up a page for your company. If your company is still without a company page, you should do so right away. Follow the instructions carefully and don't hesitate to ask question if you are not sure. Without a company page, there is no way you can establish your organization as an authority.

Apart from providing details about the identity of your company, its nature, method of operating, you shouldn't forget to upload the logo of your organization. You should create one if at all your business has none yet.

You should also know that while the page gives information about the company, it's also the means by which you share content that enhances the visibility of your brand.

Once you have a company page, it becomes easier to get across to your followers. You need to have written down your content ideas and know your schedule. The topics that you can write on based on your industry include:

- Trends
- Business related advises/recommendations
- Newsfeed from the company
- Valid opinion given by authorities in your industry.

Focused Content Marketing

Your content marketing must be focused. What's the purpose of creating content on LinkedIn when there is no direction or goal? Generally, your content should educate, inspire, or entertain. Wherever your business choose to stand, it must led by a goal or goals. Among other things, you should do the following with content marketing:

- Publish authentic information – It's essential that you look beyond the need to incorporate sales promotion into your content. While it's a give and take situation, you should be willing to give more. Publish helpful information on your company's page. You can share industry updates and events with them, introduce them to online courses – free or paid, and many more.

- Be interesting: Your target has more than enough content to deal with. Do they need more? No. What then do they need? They the kind of content that interests them. They are not asking you to turn your content to some sort of jokes, just that they need you to make it interesting to read. Add some fun, include animation, images, use cartoons in driving home your point, and many more.

- Don't be selfish: It's okay to focus on growing your page but don't be selfish. Other pages are trying to do the same thing as well. Post relevant comments on their posts, like, and share if you find it useful. When you show others that you can notice theirs, they will also pay attention to you.

- Be engaging: The level of engagement which users have with your content matters a lot. At every point in the development of your content, make sure you get your audience involved. Spur them to engage you in the comment section and be there to reply. Don't just publish and go away. Be there when they start responding.

Create a Plan that is Specific to the Newsfeed

Important information about your company or the industry you belong to are expected to be made available on your newsfeed. Apart from that you can also keep them updated about job opportunities in your industry.

You can employ the tips below to guide you in engaging users through your newsfeed:

- Share relevant information about available job opportunities.
- Introduce them to skills they can learn to improve their chances for job opportunities in your company or industry.
- Hint them on the career prospects they can gain from your company.

To have positive impact, you need to create a design for the content that you want to be sharing on your newsfeed. Not only will doing so give you a sense of direction, you gain a valid position in the mind of your users. Eventually, they would see your page as where they could get certain information related to the industry.

Be Selective with Groups Membership

You don't need to belong to every group that comes your way on LinkedIn. Before you join a group, make sure it's necessary and relevant to your market niche.

There will be a lot of groups anyway, you just need to deliberate and intentional. But how can make the right choice when you don't know what you are looking out for? So we recommend that you identify with your goals first.

Once you join a group that can offer benefits such as boosting your visibility and increasing the traffic to your page, you should also participate in the activities of the group.

You must be willing to share ideas and information as well. Don't keep anything that would help members of your group to yourself.

What should you do before you join a group?

- Check the number of users.
- Check the level of engagement which takes place among the members.

Find the information box that gives you necessary statistics about a group before you join. For the level of engagement among members, see the number of posts in the previous month. This comes with number of comments under each post.

Keep Personal Thoughts To Yourself

LinkedIn is not your usual social media sites. If you want to share connections with professionals, you must also act like a professional. How do you show that you are a professional? Your articles and comments must accent this. Your personal thoughts and messages should be kept to yourself.

It doesn't matter what your intentions are, LinkedIn is not a platform where you brag about your new house, the meal you had at a restaurant, or your new designer shoe.

Learn Patience

LinkedIn is not your usual social media platform. So, you might not always get the results you are eager to see. Learn patience. Embrace this simple truth so as not to hinder your steady growth on the platform. There will be times where the level of engagement with your post will even be below your expectations. It doesn't mean you are not saying the right thing, it doesn't even mean you are not growing. Expectations may not be achieved because you probably don't share the same time zones with your users.

It takes time –it's slow, but you need to stay visible. And don't let it be about your page alone. Attend to the needs of others as well. Make relevant comments even on the posts of your competitors.

Schedule Your Updates

You need to be careful with your approach to uploading on LinkedIn. You don't have to post all the time, stop uploading the same information over and over again.

What works on other platforms might just end up giving your negative results on LinkedIn. You won't want to be tagged a spammer. While your updates must be relevant to your industry, you need to offer fresh perspective in each update. Plus, you don't have to post every two hours of the day. Keep it to one or two and your page will be fine. And when you have nothing to upload, spend your time reading the posts of others and commenting on them.

Keep it straight and short

Don't drive your users into some bottomless pit when you post. Be straight to the point and avoid irrelevant details. This matters if you want them to interact with your posts. Apart from being relevant, you need be straight. How do you make this possible?

- Use titles.
- Use self-explanatory subheadings.
- Use bullet points or numbering.

Getting Headlining Right

Making sure your targets read your content when it appears in their newsfeeds starts with having the right headline. Not only must your headline be accurate, it must be intriguing enough to make them want to read to the end.

Be Consistent

To be visible on LinkedIn, you must be consistent. What's the ingredient for disaster on LinkedIn? Being active for a day and becoming no-where-to-be-found for a whole week. You need to be regular with your updates.

While we advise against posting almost every two hours of the day, it's okay to post once in a day.

Optimize LinkedIn Publishing Platform

You stand to gain a lot when you use LinkedIn publishing platform. Important among them is the opportunity to reach your target audience without stress as long as your content is relevant.

Even LinkedIn can decide to annotate your work, share it as well as sell its advert space on the page of your content.

Incorporate the Use of SlideShare

Your eBooks and blogs may not always meet your set expectations. You can then use other feature like SlideShare which LinkedIn offers. SlideShare helps you to add visual content to your content with ease.

How do you do this? You must have created a page for your company on LinkedIn, then link the SlideShare page to company's page. Once you do this, every document you create on SlideShare will be shown on your LinkedIn account.

But you must have incorporated the right visual content that can attract high-level interaction. We are yet to see anyone whose senses don't interact with a well created visual. The content could be a simplification of a topic of interest in your industry. What matters is readability and great visual.

You shouldn't miss out on this opportunity. This could be your way to beating your optimization using content marketing strategy.

Chapter 7:
How to Boost Your Connections

LinkedIn is focused on helping you build a network of those you already know and those you are interested in knowing. What more can do but to join a platform which boasts about half a billion users spread across over 200 countries? This is contained in the report of *About LinkedIn, 2019*.

Despite this revelation, doesn't it surprise you that many users still find it complicated? For many, including marketers, it is the need to increase their connections that poses a challenge. Have you also wondered who you should connect with and who you shouldn't? Unfortunately, spending your time thinking about this could hinder you from boosting your connections on the platform.

And really, no one is to be blamed. What happens after exhausting your contact list? You need to be careful not to invite those who are not relevant to your industry to connect with you. Moreover, as a marketer, you should be more interested in those who can eventually convert to buyers or those with promising chance of leading you to them.

Thus, in this chapter, we will look into helpful techniques that can boost your connections. But before then, let's consider the degrees of connections available on LinkedIn.

Degrees of LinkedIn Connection

Your network, popularly known a connection, entails 1st-degree, 2nd-degree, and 3rd-degree. Like sending friend request or accepting one on Facebook, LinkedIn uses connection. And the way you interact with someone on LinkedIn depends on the degree of connection you have with them. So, let's talk about these degrees below:

- 1st-Degree Connections: In this category are those you connected with directly. It's either because you accepted your invitation to connect or the other way round. On their profile, you will spot the 1st-degree label. You can also send them a message via the platform as well.

- 2nd-Degree Connections: Those in this category share a connection with your 1st- degree connections. On their profile or when searched for using the search too, you will find the label. You can use the InMail feature to contact them.

- 3rd-Degree Connections: Those in this category share a connection with your 2nd- degree connections. On their profile or when searched for using the search too, you will find the label.

How do you connect with these individuals?

1. When the full name of an individual is on display, you will be able to send an invitation to connect by hitting the Connect button.
2. If you are only able to see the first name of an individual on display, you can't send an invitation to connect using the Connect button. You can only get across to such using the InMails feature.

- Group Members: This category belong to the same group as you. The profile of a member you share a group with will indicate a highlight page that lets you see your mutual connection. You can connect with them straight from the group or send them messages via LinkedIn.

Is Having a Large Network Significant?

LinkedIn grants up to 30,000 connections. But this doesn't mean you must attain this standard before you can access all the benefits the network provides. Your goal, however, should be to make above 500 connections so as to bank on a complete profile in the view of LinkedIn.

So, why is having a large network important? Some of the reasons that support this need are below:

- It enhances your LinkedIn search results: Unless a recruiter running a search related to you is using LinkedIn Recruiter or inputting your full name in the search box, results will only show individuals who are connected to the researcher using the degrees of connections on the platform.

- It doesn't matter whether these users are 3rd – degree connections, you have a higher chance of appearing in search results if you have a significant number of connections. This is because LinkedIn does not identify users using the degree of connections. So, what we are trying to say is that your level of visibility will be very low if you don't have a significant level of connections.

- With a significant level of connections comes an increased level of reach for your content. How does this work? When you upload a post, LinkedIn notifies your connections and this means the higher your number, the more the level of engagement you are bound to generate. Ultimately, your content could be featured on LinkedIn Pulse if the level of engagement can't be ignored by LinkedIn.

- More views to your profile: People view your profile as soon as they connect with you. Don't you do the same? What happens if your profile is buyer-focused? You have a chance of converting someone to a buyer there. Some people get as much as 500 or 1000 views in a week. Imagine what their numbers would be in 90 days and imagine what this implies if you are a marketer?

- Increased Endorsements: Endorsements are like badge of honors. Not only does it boost your credibility and make your profile look appealing, it helps to draw the attention of recruiters who are looking for raw talents. Without a significant number of connections, there is no way you can have enough individuals in your network to endorse you for one skill or the other.

Having looked into some of the reasons you need to increase your LinkedIn connections, let's lead you through the categories of people you can connect with.

Who Are the People to Connect With?

Professionals You Are Familiar With

In this arm are those people you have worked with in the past or are still working with. They may also be those you have met at events and had a small conversation with. They already are part of your physical professional life, so it's not wrong to connect with them online. They know what you do and you know what they do and it becomes easier to endorse each other on LinkedIn.

Professionals You Love to Meet or Know

These are the ones whom although you have not met them, you have developed interest in meeting due to their profile. It could even be that you have heard them speak at an occasion related to your industry and you would like to walk in their footsteps. With great wealth of experience that makes them stand out, these professionals could end up being your mentors or employees later.

Family, Friends and Acquaintances

Now, it doesn't matter whether the ones in this group are in the same industry with you or not. Apart from the fact that those from a different industry can help you gain perspective about an industry you are not in, they can always be resourceful to your professional and career growth in the long run. They include friends, families, old class mates, colleague at work, and so on.

Those with Many Connections

Don't overlook anyone on LinkedIn. These individuals have a lot of connections due to the nature of their jobs or it could just be who they are. And you never can tell, they may be the connection between you and some of other persons you need to connect with or even the company you need to access.

Those with Prospects

Some individuals may not have the kind of glory you look for in a connection, don't overlook their prospects. They are probably those who are just getting started in the industry or have newly launched a business but would love to connect as well. Since you have no idea what the future holds, don't hesitate to send them an invite.

Those with Attractive Skills

No matter how good you are in your field of expertise, someone has unique skills which you are going to need in some future time. If you find the profile of such, connect with them. Maybe he or she is an expert programmer or has a vast knowledge on an industry-related topic; don't take it for granted. You never can tell when you would need him or her to save the day for you.

Your Consistent Critic

Being criticized is not really a crime, if it's constructively passed by the critic. Your critic could include those who wouldn't take less from you, who push you without letting emotion get in the way except when you achieve a set goal.

And what happens when you fail to achieve a set goal? They may say things that could hurt you but you should be grateful about constructive criticism if you want to have a career growth. So, don't hesitate to connect with these individuals if you have a chance to.

With the list of people you could connect with has been set, let's talk about the techniques you could use to increase your connections.

Design Your Connection Requests

Although LinkedIn makes suggestions to you about individuals you can connect with, try to connect with four or more people at a time.

However, don't just hit the button. Doing this will only direct a general message but you can do it better. What you can do is to visit the profile page of the individual to use the connect button available there. Through this method, you will be able to include a personal message in your connection request.

Drafting a message that fits the person you are trying to connect with, you should answer the following in your message:

- How you know the individual.
- Where you have met.
- The reason you are trying to reconnect.

For instance, if you are interested in connecting with an individual, you could draft your message as this:

"I have been following some of your uploads for some weeks now. While I do not always agree with your views, I have found some of them to be resourceful. I look forward to connecting with you. Thanks."

This won't take much of your time. In fact, the connection requests you sent have a higher chance of being honored and given attention to.

Connect With Those You Meet Physically

Beyond all the features that LinkedIn and other social media platforms offer, physical connection will remain relevant. It will always be a vital aspect of networking. So, you should build a physical relationship with your connections as much as possible.

Attend industry-related events that are also attending. Attend professional meetings that is open to members of the public, and don't be too shy to introduce yourself to them should you have a chance to get close. It doesn't even matter where you meet them – it could be at the grocery.

Beyond LinkedIn, you should also network in the real world. You don't have to wait till you meet someone you connected with via LinkedIn. When you go to the store, at the mall, and other public places, you should introduce yourself to people and once they introduce their names too, search for their profile on LinkedIn. Attach a message to remind them of how you met, they would be more willing to accept your request to connect.

Set Goals

With a goal in mind, it's quite easier to achieve any given task. Set a target for yourself –maybe to get 5 connections a week or about 20 in a month.

Mind you, you should be realistic with your goals. And don't be desperate so you won't end up flouting the rules of what is acceptable and what is not on LinkedIn. Don't forget that above all else, quality is highly priced above quantity. Plus, don't be disappointed if some invitations are not accepted. Some people are just like that – they won't accept invitation from people they haven't met before. The best thing to do is to focus on what you have set to achieve on LinkedIn. One thing you should know is that when you have also invested rightly into giving value, the right connections will start sending request instead.

Post Content Each Day

Gaining visibility on LinkedIn requires that you remain active online. Mind you, you should be professional about this – it is not your typical social media site where you post irrelevancies.

Except it adds value, don't post it. And before you talk about what you do and incorporate a CTA into your content, make sure you have created value first.

Consistency is key. When you remain in the feeds of your connections, they will eventually get to like, leave comments, and share. When there is a high-level engagement, it gives you a strong credibility in the eyes of existing connections and targets.

Include your LinkedIn profile URL in your Email Signature

Your LinkedIn profile brings you a lot of benefits that you can't afford to miss out on any. Among other things, your LinkedIn profile is your CV, testimonial, statement of purpose, social management certificate and proof that you are what you say you are. It even says more than you can think of. So, why not direct your potential employee to your LinkedIn profile instead of Facebook?

How can you do this without stress?

Copy your LinkedIn vanity URL – a clickable link that's quite easy to find. Go to the info page and click the gear icon by the side of your LinkedIn URL. As soon as the first page comes up, find the Public Profile URL page to make adjustments. And once you have the vanity URL, add it to your email signature. With this incorporation, it becomes easier for anyone to connect with you. Don't forget to add your business card as well.

Join groups

There are a lot of groups related to your industry that you can become a part of. But don't be in a hurry to join any if you are not sure you would be active.

Eventually, when you do, be active. On the other hand, how does joining groups benefit you? Groups could be used for executing market research, you enjoy the opportunity to engage those within your market niche, and you can as well post links to your updates with the groups. When you do this with a level of professionalism as well as consistency, they would be more willing to send invitations to you. You might even find a business partner via the run a groups you belong to. And you don't have to go for groups with large members only. You should be willing to start with small ones too.

Meanwhile, you could take another step to create a group by yourself.

To take it further, you can create a group of your own. But that's when you really have something to offer your group members. People who join groups have expectations, you shouldn't disappoint them. When you establish it that you are expert by what you do, you will have a lot of connections especially as they already know who you are and the types of content you upload.

Input Keywords in Your profile

So that people won't have a problem finding you on LinkedIn, you need to input the right keywords into your profile. There are strategic parts you should pay attention to while building your profile. They are headline, experience, and summary.

Since the sections above can be searched using the search box, it's easier to get found when you use the right keywords related to your industry when filling them. Please, make sure you are creative. And then, you should optimize all the characters allowed.

Share Relevant Content on LinkedIn's Publishing Platform

If you are interested in demonstrating yourself as an industry expert, you should make use of LinkedIn's publishing platform to create and share relevant and useful posts.

Usually, three of your posts will be displayed on your profile. Apart from that, any content you upload will be viewed by the users on your platform apart from those you are connected to. With this, your level of exposure can increase across broad.

Don't forget everything we have discussed about staying visible through consistent posting. Also, we also talked about the types of content you can optimize and how you can incorporate visuals like animations, infographics as well as SlideShare.

What's more? Make sure your every content you post is recent and factual. In case you are unable to publish fresh content, you can edit and repurpose your old blogs.

Use Images

Do you still remember the power images? Incorporate images as much as you can, it won't hurt. This greatly boosts your chance of getting good engagements on every of your posts. Prospective connections would be curious to go through your profile when they see how you incorporate images into your content marketing strategy.

So, don't just post links on your page, add images too.

Keep Engaging Your Present Connections

Frequently, make it a habit to check your newsfeed to like, comment, and share uploads of your connections. Strike a relationship with your new connections by commenting on their updates. Not only that, you take part of the popular conversations going on in your industry.

This helps you to be gain more visibility to a large number of individuals. And when you are able to stimulate the interest of others, they will be eager to send you invitation to connect.

Leverage Other Social Platforms in Promoting Your LinkedIn URL

You should take advantage of other social media platforms in promoting your LinkedIn URL. Every social site gives you a chance to include you bio, and this is an opportunity to drive connections to your LinkedIn profile.

You could do it in a more stimulating dimension. You could post link in a tweet, photo, video, or status update on the same site. There is nothing wrong in doing this, so use it judiciously. However, you should make sure you have claimed your vanity URL so as to get this done.

Make Use of your Email Contacts

Have you received some message that reads like "Tony would like to connect with you on LinkedIn"? If yes, we can bet you wondered why Tony would love to connect with you. Isn't it?

Well, that's what happened when you import your email contacts on LinkedIn. Once it brings in all the available contacts, each would begin to get a connection request from you.

While you might find this kind of method annoying, you shouldn't neglect the fact that you could get a good number of connections through this. So, include as many emails as possible that you have at your disposal. It's possible that you must have sent them messages at one point or the other in the past. So, it shouldn't be a problem when they get connection request from you. And you should know that it's possible that not everyone on your list has LinkedIn account. So, don't be surprised when you fail to meet all the expectations you have set to build your connections fast.

Meanwhile, if you have a problem with sending a connection request to those you have no interest in connecting with, you can screen your list before the generic message is sent to them.

Send Connect Requests to LIONS

LION refers to LinkedIn Open Networkers. This is a group of individuals who have no problem with random people sending them connection invitation. This means they will accept your invite.

Although LIONS may differ in quality, don't hesitate to connect with them. Who knows, having them as your first degree connection will grant you access to their second connections which may eventually be important to you.

How do you find LIONS on LinkedIn?

Input this same keyword in the search box in the form of LIONS or L.I.O.N, and these individuals will show up in search results. On your own part too, you can include LION in your profile so that those looking for networkers can find you as well.

Connect with Individuals Who Check Out Your Profile

LinkedIn notifies you of people who viewed your profile, don't just view the list and move on. We can bet they must have viewed your profile for one reason or the other – they came across you via keyword search, was recommended to them by LinkedIn, or they found your post. So, they decided to check your profile. Don't take LinkedIn's revelation for granted.

Take a step further to connect with them. Since they already viewed your profile, you have a better chance of being accepted to connect when you send them invite.

The same happens when you view the profile of others. They take it as a prompt and are encouraged to want to connect with you. So, don't be surprised if someone whose profile you viewed eventually sends you a request. It's a good way to build connections too.

Publish Videos

This feature is still new and many users are yet to key into it. Besides, the algorithm is yet to give it any priority. But don't wait till that happens before you key into it. Take it as part of your content marketing strategy that can help your secure a good position before it becomes overcrowded.

As a marketer, take your chance and begin to attract your targets with the right video content. This is one of the chances you need to take to boost the visibility of your company and its brand. There can be no better time than to do it now.

Chapter 8:
Steps to Creating Successful Ads on LinkedIn

LinkedIn is a great social media networking platform for like-minded professionals. But do you know that it offers you a great opportunity to create ads. So, if you have been creating ads successful ads on platforms like Facebook or Instagram, you can as well optimize the same on LinkedIn.

Therefore, this chapter will discuss how to create your first ad campaign on LinkedIn. Are you ready?

How does LinkedIn Ads Work?

There are two steps involved in ads. They are developing of your campaign and creation of the ad. Let's discuss them below:

Developing Your Campaign

Unlike the typical LinkedIn platform where you connect with professionals like you, you get to develop and create your ad on the LinkedIn Marketing Solutions platform. Once you navigate to this page, you should select the *Create Ad* button.

Following that, you will be requested to open a Campaign Manager account where you will include the page of your company if you have one. After, you will be required to include your billing data if you are yet to do so. Note that this is necessary if you must unlock your account.

Through the campaign manager or via your dashboard, a button for you to create campaign will be seen. Click on this and you will be introduced to a page where you can begin the development of your campaign.

Before you begin the development of your campaign, you should select a campaign group and then name your campaign. The goal of the Campaign group is to assist you in arranging your campaign. And if you don't want a new group, you can stick to the default group.

After doing the campaign group selection, you should now proceed to select a campaign objective.

Pick your objective

What is meant by an ad objective is the action you want those who view your ad to take. LinkedIn offers you three motifs that you can pick from:

- Consideration
- Awareness
- Conversion

Under these motifs are objectives that you can also select from. They are:

- Site Traffic: If your ad creation intent is to drive traffic to your landing pages and sites, this should be an objective you should take. According to LinkedIn suggestion, this is the kind of campaign that you should use when attempting to create awareness for your brand.

- Video views: The objective of this is to help you drive exposure to videos through those who are likely to interact with them.

- Engagement: This goal is necessary if you are interested in enhancing the level of engagement which followers have with your company page.

- Lead Generation: With this goal, you will be able to set a form for the purpose of lead generation. It will be shown to LinkedIn users who have the potential to engage with the form.

Having determined the objective of your ad campaigns, it's time to choose the targets of your ads.

Select Your Target Audience

Targeting the individuals who view your ad will aid the actualization of your campaign objective. You should know that the level of performance which your ad has speaks well of how relevant and specific your campaign is. And you have a chance to target your audience using different categories made available by LinkedIn.

While you don't have to use all the options at your disposal, you should ensure that your ad is relevant to the audience it is directed to. This is to ensure that you get the best return from your investment. Among other things, you will be required to pick the language in which you want your ads to appear. There are about 20 languages supported by LinkedIn, so it's possible to target any category of audience.

Mind you, you can only pick one location for your ad. So, you should be specific – direct your ad to the location that's valuable to your business.

Then you should pick "+ Add new targeting criteria" where you have the criteria discussed below to pick from:

- Company: should your target have a specified employer, this makes it possible to target it directly by employing its name. Meanwhile, you may not need to be specific, so LinkedIn gives options distributed into sectors like Banking, Health, Insurance as well as the size of the company.

- Interests: This offers you a great opportunity to target those who share the same interest with you. Among them are people who are in the same industry, belong to the same group, and/or follow the same expert. In addition, if they have interest in the same topic as you, it becomes easier to target them.

- Demographics: This option allows you to target audience who belong to a set group, gender, and age.

- Work Experience: This is part of audience demographics which you can use to target those with a particular work experience. For example, if your product is for doctors of diabetic patient, being specific about this in your ad creation will save you more time and money. You can also select specific years of experience, job titles, and level to give your ad a clearer perspective. Apart from that, you can also target individuals with specific set of skills. So, it's okay to consider the aspect that your targets fall into so that you can better direct your ad to do an effective campaign for you.

- Education: With LinkedIn ad, you can also target individuals using the level of education or educational history. It's that easy. For example, if you are directing your campaign to schools, you can sue degree or level of study to create a more specific campaign.

If you have been able to set a targeting criteria that works for you, you can save it as the template for future uses. You can also extend your campaign reach by including those who share certain similarities with your target audience. Once this is done, you should determine the format of your ad.

Determine the Ad Format

The format of LinkedIn that you pick from include the following:

- Text ads: These kind of ads are displayed at the top of LinkedIn page and it can also show up right beneath the section of those you may know shown you by LinkedIn. Creating this kind of ad is not difficult – you can use cost per a given number of impressions or cost per click to set it up. Mind you, the kind of texts you select could make or mar your ad conversion rates.

- One image ads: These are single images that are displayed as organic content on LinkedIn's newsfeed.

- Job placement ads: These ads are shown only on the desktop version of LinkedIn. Jobs available can be advertised while using the data of the profile user to personalize it.

- Carousel ads: These ads have two images or more shown on the newsfeed.

- Message ads/Sponsored InMails: These categories are sent to the LinkedIn inbox of your targets. Incorporated into these are CTA click, body of the text, customized greeting, and a link which leads to site or landing page. Meanwhile, you will be charged by LinkedIn for each unit delivered on your behalf.

- Follower ads: These types are targeted at followers. The aim is to promote the LinkedIn page using the data of followers. Mind you, this can only be viewed by users of LinkedIn via desktop.

Before you select any kind of ads format, you should check the *projected results box* at the right at the right-hand side of the page. This grants you the opportunity to evaluate the characteristics of your campaign such as bid, budget, and campaign, among others.

It's important to note them because you have to consider the budget you have before picking a suitable ad that meets your campaign needs.

Placement

Following the above, you should decide whether you want your ad to be placed on the LinkedIn Audience Network – a network that offers more exposure than reach or not. But then, you should note that you will only be able to pick this network based on the kind of ad you pick for use.

If you decide to go with the network, you have the chance to take out applications, categories, and websites you don't want.

Ascertain your Budget & Schedule

Before you pick any ad category, you should consider your budget and the scheduling options that is suitable for you.

Budget

We recommend that you only place a daily budget for the kind of ad that is okay for your budget. And more importantly, you should test the viability of one campaign before you put your resources into it. It doesn't matter if you have the money to spend on it if at the end of the day it's not relevant to your targets.

That's why you must have known who needs your ad before you select the specifications for your campaign. Imagine having to invest so much by placing an amazing bid on ad to be shown to brides-to-be in CA. And when you failed to meet your targeted sales a baker, you carried out a research and realized that there are quite a lot of students in your location who needs your cake. So, as you can see, it would be great to know these things in advance so that you won't end up budgeting for an ad campaign directed to the wrong people.

Although LinkedIn offers you the capacity to reach a given market, you should spend time doing your research. It would save you from spending needlessly on ads. Don't you think so?

Schedule

It is important to have a schedule for the commencement of your campaign. You have a chance to have it displayed over and over again around the clock or just at the end of a given time.

Type of Bid

When it comes to picking your bid, you have three options to select from:

- Automated bid: When you select this, you grant LinkedIn the freedom to charge the amount that will help you realize the objective of your campaign in terms of impression, or clicks, or impressions.

- Maximum (CPM) pay-per-1,000 Impressions bid: With this kind of option, you only get charged when a total of 1000 targets on the platform see your ad. Please note that this will not be available if you are not using the LinkedIn Audience Network option.

- Maximum (CPC) or cost-per-click bid: The implication of this is that you will pay each time a person clicks on your ad. Using the competition that surrounds your ad, LinkedIn will suggest bid ranges to you. You should know the higher the percentage of advertisers competing for a similar campaign, the higher your bid has to be and that's the maximum you will be charged by LinkedIn. And in case your present rate is below your peak bid, you will only be expected to pay for the current bid placed.

Deciding could be complicated but you should decide with the end goal of you ads campaign at the back of your mind.

Hence, you should ask yourself the following:

- Is your goal about ensuring as many targets as possible view your ads?

- Or to help them with a branding campaign or a similar intent? CPM could be your ideal choice.

- Is your goal is to ensure that a good number of targets click on your ads and eventually generate new leads or drive traffic to your landing page or site? Then, CPC could be your ideal choice.

Above all else, be willing to experiment a little. The place to begin with is the suggestions made available to you by LinkedIn. Apart from its suggestions, you should think of the time that your targets are usually available and active online. It is at this time that you should be ready to place higher bids on your ads.

And more importantly, be sure that LinkedIn is the right place to place your ad. To be sure, you can experiment with other social media platforms before you finally settle down to any.

Tracking Your Conversions

At this point, you have the chance to include conversion tracking in your campaign. This is necessary so that you can monitor and measure what targets do once they click on your ads.

You might think it's not important as soon as you have been able to put your ads campaign in place but you never can tell the values it would bring to the direction of your conversion goals.

To do this, select *"+ Add conversions."* Once you do, a new window will appear for you to input a name for your conversion. After which you will have to pick your ideal settings and how you intend to track the conversions that occur.

Is that all, no? Don't be in a hurry to save because you won't be able to change your ad format and objective once you do. So, you should take your time to go over your selections before you take the next step.

Building Up Your Ad(s)

When you are done selecting the basic ingredients of your ad, you will be required to begin its development and how you want LinkedIn to display it as well as its variations if you have created two or more ads all together.

To do this, select *Create New Ad* following which a screen will pop-up. On the screen, you will develop an ad copy attached with a given image while addressing other option s as necessary.

The important things which you need to note are:

- Ad image: In the preceding paragraph, we talked about having a given image. Well, this is the work of art that will viewed by the target audience of your ad. You can upload this as a .png or .jpg file and should be 2MB or less. In terms of piels, it should be 100 x 100.

- Ad headline: your ad headline is the basic message of your created ad. The limit is 25 characters.

- Ad description: your ad description accents what you are trying to draw attention to and it can be as long as 75 characters. However, you need to make sure your description is relevant and of high-quality.

- Destination URL: Upon clicking on your ad, it should be possible to direct your targets to your site or landing page. This is the work of URL. Be sure your URL is correct.

When you are done filling these requirements, you will be able to view your details in the Preview Box. And upon selecting *Create*, you will be redirected to the previous Campaign manager screen where you can develop extra ads, do review, and present your order.

Please note that your created ad will also be reviewed by LinkedIn, so don't worry if you don't see your ad immediately.

Meanwhile, you could make unique ad for each of the personality you are targeting in your ad. All you have to do is tweak the copy that's to go with each. Now, let's look into some copywriting tips useful for LinkedIn ads.

Include a CTA (Call-to-Action)

Including CTA into your copy is a tool that helps to spur your targets to take action. You shouldn't create an inactionable ad. Your CTA is there to help you urge them to act. Examples of CTA which we can bet you must have come across are:

- "Download the free book now."
- "Add to Cart."

It makes no sense to write a copy without initiating action.

Give Value

Your targets want to know what is in it for them. And you should state this early enough in your headline and/or the first line in your description. You could include lines like "Offer ends in 24Hours / Shop now and get 30% discount." Your targets will be more willing to click on an ad that offers specific value than the one that failed to do so.

Testing

You should test your ad copy so as not to end up spending on an ad that won't meet your expectation. It's best to know before you put so much hope on it. It's your chance to experiment with different images and copies in your ads. And really, there is crime in knowing what attracts your audience before you go ahead.

Evaluating your LinkedIn Ad Campaign

It is important to evaluate your ad campaign. Until you do so, you are not done. LinkedIn has made provisions for tools through the Campaign Manager Board where you can monitor the progress of your campaign.

On the dashboard of Campaign Manager, you will be able to see the various chats that measures how each of your ad is doing. The features which are used to measure the progress are clicks, click-through-rate, and expenditures.

The graphs by the end of the dashboard is also there for you to evaluate the conversations which targets are having with your ad. Having known how to set up LinkedIn campaigns, how do you optimize them to ensure great performance?

Optimizing Your Ad Campaigns

Is it possible to boost the performance of your ads campaign? It's possible especially as platform, content, and audience are bound to go through changes. Sometimes, an ad campaign could be doing less than it ought to and you would want to improve the level of performance. Some of the methods you can use to optimize your ad campaign are considered below:

Check the CTR of Ad Campaign

Checking the CTR of your ads campaign will show you the ones that are performing and the ones which are not. When you notice that one is doing better than the other, it's advisable to put the rest on hold.

To help you, LinkedIn will always let you the ones that are doing less. But instead of putting more resources on them, you should rather concentrate on the one which is bringing you good return on investment.

Change a Variable

We advise against totally putting an end to any ad campaign that is not performing at its best rate. Perhaps, what you need to do is try out some variation for the existing ad. You could change the image, remove some words from the copy or description, update bid, and change the features of those it should target. You should only do these one at a time so as to determine which is working and that which is not.

Frequently Update your Audience Attributes

Don't ignore the new perspective that may pop-up about your targets each month. That is why you need to carry out audience research constantly. Once there are changes, don't hesitate to effect necessary changes on your ads.

Measuring Your Ad leads using Post-Click Reporting

The fact an ad is performing doesn't mean it would direct the ideal traffic to your site or landing page. Since LinkedIn won't tell you this or give you any number, it's your duty to find out using Post-Click Reporting.

This is possible through *gated* forms and offer. How can you determine this? With gated form and offer, you provide your targets with a content in the way of lead form. Through this form, you can get the information which you need to determine whether an individual is a viable lead or not. We recommend that you link the form with the CRM software used by your company so that the sales unit can take effective action as soon as the data comes in.

Meanwhile, this is no reason to neglect other useful data about your ad campaigns. You need to also see if your ads bring you qualified traffic and if the users are becoming clients already. If any of that is not happening, then it's time to alter you campaign.

There is no point in spending more on an ad which has only been able to get you deals of 20-50 people. Meanwhile, it has been created to focus on people working in companies with 500-700 each.

So far, we have examined the options available to you when targeting audience for your business. You have the chance to also alter your choice if an ad is not performing as it should. Above all, you should know that LinkedIn ad campaigns is a great opportunity to drive audience and traffic to your site among over 610 million users on the platform. So, you should spend time researching and testing so as to create effective ads. You have the chance to test and see what will work and what won't and even after creating and launching; the results are available to help you run better ads.

Chapter 9:
Guide to Creating a LinkedIn Marketing Funnel

Being a platform for professionals that boasts of about 610 million users, you need not be told that LinkedIn is a platform where you can get significant leads that will transform your sales. But then, it doesn't just happen because you want to, guides are involved.

Essentially, you need to understand how to draw prospects in. at this point, your marketing funnel has a major role to play. Before we continue, we need to consider what a marketing funnel means.

Funnels: What You Should Know

The intent of directing those who click your ads is for them to take meaningful action. It could be signing up, adding a product to the cart, or filling a form. Once any of those actions and others are carried out, that's a conversion for you. That is, rather than just looking around, the target converts through the action taken.

But did it just happen? No, your target went through a funnel before successfully converting.

Stages of a Funnel

Your target go through a process from the moment he or she comes into contact with what you are marketing. The only difference is that, based on market niche, personality of buyer, and the category of product/services offered, the road taken may be different.

And then, it is expected that you would have had a clear business goal, defined marketing strategy, and defined audience before you create a marketing funnel. These are necessary in order to enhance the success of your business.

While a marketing funnel may contain many stages, the basic ones are considered below:

- Awareness: At this stage, the prospect just found out about the product, service, or solution you offer for his/her problem.

- Decision: Following awareness, the prospect will try to decide whether to choose or ignore what you offer.

- Action: Having made a decision to accept your offer, the prospect is expected to take an action here either buy filling a form or signing up to your newsletter for more information.

- Retention: At this stage you, you have the prospect as client on the list of company.

Having examined the stages in the marketing funnel that leads a prospect to becoming a significant client, we will now talk about how to create an effective marketing funnel for your company Having covered the stages in a funnel, let's move on to how you can create a successful marketing funnel on LinkedIn for your business.

Step 1: Identify Your Prospects and Connect

Identifying who your prospects are and connecting with them on LinkedIn is necessary. After all, getting to more about your ideal client is quite necessary to eventually converting him or her.

To start with, you should find answers to the questions below:

- Who is an ideal client? Is he or she on LinkedIn?
- What is the basic language of the industry, business, or company he or she belongs?
- What type of issues does he or she deal with?

Following the above, you need to ruminate over the title of decision makers in the companies you are targeting. It needs to be the kind of person you are searching for. For example: Director of Purchases and Acquisition, Chief Marketing Officer, and so on.

You can also take a step further by locating the industries they are situated, the country or city they live in, and so on. With this data at your disposal, you carry out advanced search that's offered by LinkedIn.

LinkedIn Advanced Search

Once you have precise data at your disposal, LinkedIn can help you locate significant prospects using LinkedIn Advanced Search. This search offers screen data.

Let's assume that your clients are Chief Marketing Officers. All you have to do is input the same description in the search box, then select *People* as your option. Then, in order to avoid results of people you are already connected with, don't select 1st-degree connections.

Other options you can use on this tool to further keep your search focused are immediate organization of prospect, location, and others. You can save the results made available to you by selecting *Create a search alert* in the *Saved Searches* box which can be found in the right hand side of your results page.

You should incorporate this so as to receive notification from LinkedIn as soon as new members with the same results join the platform.

As you can see, it makes looking for new leads effortless.

Send a Personalized Request to Connect

As soon as you find prospects, don't hesitate to connect with them. And as we earlier covered in previous chapters, don't send generic messages to prospective connections. Make sure you personalize it. This is necessary so as not to leave your prospects wondering why you want to connect. It's best to answer the question even before the think it necessary to wonder or ask.

And make sure the message is client-focused. Make it seem like it's about them and not you.

More than anything, sending personalized message helps you to build a professional page. The moment you send a generic message, the prospect may decide to ignore your request and this comes with the option of selecting *I don't know this person*. Why does this matter? If you end up having a pile of this on your account, you are likely to be restricted by LinkedIn. It's not good for you or your business.

Step 2: Engage and Develop a Relationship with your Connections

Once a person accepts your invitation to connect, set in motion a process that will help you connect with him or her. Remember, you need to leave a lasting impression in the first attempt so that the connection would also be more willing with develop a relationship with you.

Don't throw your promotions into their face. That's a simple way to tell them that you care less about what they do and what matters to them. Believe it, you are not going to make it far if that's how you intend to strike a relationship with your connections.

First, you should thank them for accepting your request. It tells them you value their willingness. Then, you can take a step further by asking them a question relevant to them. The implication of this is that you must gone through their profile in order to ask the right question.

Be like the marketers who amass connections without ever trying to start a conversation. It's funny that they are still lost on why they are yet to have any convert among their connections. The same thing applies to attending networking events, collecting business cards here and there, and failing to call the numbers. At the end of the day, you are in the same boat with those who didn't attend at all.

Step 3: Give Value & Build Trust

You should know that striking a relationship is beyond sending a thank you message and asking about how they are doing. You need to be consistent by sending more messages that are of value to your connections.

When you post valuable content, job opportunities, and events that they can benefit from on your page, they begin to trust you as a resourceful person. You can even take a step further by sending opportunities to them privately.

Mind you, you don't have to necessarily be the one who created the content. When you find a content and it happens to be valuable, let your connections also see it. No one cares if it's your creative effort or someone else's, as long as it helps your connections in solving one problem or the other.

Be reminded once again that you have ample time to pitch your business. Start first by building relationship through trust and offering of value. Until you create value, don't advertise.

When thinking of direction of the content you want to share on LinkedIn, you should ask yourself the questions below:

- What are they interest in?
- What is important to them?
- What are the challenges they are dealing with?

Step 4: Strengthen Relationships

There are quite a number of things you can to do to strengthen relationships with your connections. Remember we talked about offering value earlier. So, you can start with teaching them something, offering your assistant in achieving an opportunity that means so much to them, and contributing to their activities on LinkedIn.

Find below ideas that can help you strengthen relationships with connections.

- Leave valuable comments on what they share on their page. Don't forget to share if it's worth it.
- Recommend connections that would be of value to them.
- Share relevant content from you or your connections that can help them in their work with them.
- Ask questions that can help you get to know them.
- Share content that can help you start a conversation with them regularly.
- Take a step forward to know them by following them on other social media platforms as well.

The above are not too much to embrace if you are serious about building a relationship. You must understand that some people won't give you attention until they notice that you care. To remain in their face and mind, start with offering value and developing trust alongside.

Step 5: Engage in Conversation Offline

In the process of attempting to take them to the last stage of your marketing funnel, you should have an offline conversation with your connection. You don't need to do this all the time with every connection but if you can, it's very useful.

Let's say you are trying to pitch painting services to someone and will like to convert them to a client, you need to build offline conversation into your strategy. On the other hand, if it's an interest in taking trainings online, you don't need to go for having online conversation.

Generally speaking still, situation arises in marketing where you just have to take the conversation offline. As long as you have spent your time establishing the building blocks of a quality relationship, asking for an offline meeting won't be tagged as overstepping.

And don't get it wrong, offline doesn't have to be a lunch or dinner at a fancy restaurant. It could just putting calls through once in a while or a short meeting.

During your offline conversations, you should listen to them. See, it's about them. That's why a good marketer is a good listener. Get to know what they are facing and offer them solution only when it is right. They jump into their moment of revelation, let them have the chance to talk when it's their turn.

Meanwhile, you don't have to follow the marketing funnel strictly. Some clients already know what they want, and it wouldn't be a problem pitching to them during a second interaction. As long as you are sure that's what works best for your business, don't hesitate to take your chance.

At the moment, there is no such platform for professionals and growth-inclined individuals. So, with the right mindset, you are bound to win. LinkedIn is a great source of gaining qualified leads for your business as long as you know how identify prospects. There are sources in the previous chapters that can help you through.

Chapter 10:
Important Tools and Apps to Optimize

There are important LinkedIn marketing tools that are available to you as an entrepreneur, business manager, and individual to enhance your marketing strategy.

LinkedIn is a platform where you can forge lasting corporate and personal relationships. On the same platform, you can find individuals to collaborate with towards a business or project. However, if you are a newbie on LinkedIn or you have been there for some time and don't know how to navigate your way, it might be hard to optimize the resources made available.

The marketing tools made available by LinkedIn re important if you intend to take your marketing strategy to the next level. Thus, in this chapter, we will examine the apps and tools that can help make your efforts on LinkedIn more efficient. With these tools, you can see the world from a unique perspective and ultimately, achieve measurable result.

Are you ready?

LinkedIn Sales Navigator

If you are interested in boosting your sales with LinkedIn, this is for you. LinkedIn sales navigator is a tool that serves as a bridge between sellers and buyers in a unique way.

The important features which you can find on LinkedIn Sales Navigator include:

- Tools for building relationships that brings you closer to the successful sales.

- Insights from sales that can help you make informed decision on behalf of your business.

- Sales Navigator helps you identify ideal prospect for the product or service you are trying to offer.

The moment you start receiving recommendations, the tools offered by Sales Navigator can be used to access them and also sell to them.

Mind you, Sales Navigator does offer guarantee that your sales and revenue will move to a position that you have never had. It just one of the tools whose features you can use to get started.

Webfluential

Your business strategy may require you to connect with influencers on LinkedIn. Webfluential is one marketing tool which you can use. Through this tool, you can connect with top influencers in your industry in order to use their influence to build a great reach for your brand.

With Webfluential, you can locate the right match for your business. Once you do, let them help you build an effective brand on your behalf.

LinkedIn Plugins

Looking for a LinkedIn functionality for incorporation into your website or landing page? LinkedIn plugins come is available for your use.

There are many plugins on LinkedIn that many business owners and marketers are allowing to slip through their hands. These plugins are direct methods of enhancing sales and some of them are listed below:

- Company Profile
- Follow Company
- Share
- Alumni Tool
- Member Profile
- LinkedIn AutoFill
- Company Insider
- Job and Job Titles You are Interest In.

For example, if you want visitors on your website to see the profile of your business, you can add the Company Profile plug in. having done that, visitors will be able to see what your business represents. It's also a way to let them catch a glimpse of those you have affiliation with if you are an affiliate marketer.

Mind you, LinkedIn Plugins can only help in sales increase; we don't recommend them as the most effective tool for sales growth.

eLink Pro

eLink Pro is a tool that evangelizes the notion that if you check the profile of someone on LinkedIn, he/she will do the same. This sounds true but there is a challenge that comes with it. The challenge is having the time to go through every profile you actually desire to.

And what can you if it's actually the profile of qualified prospects? Don't worry, you have eLink Pro.

With this tool, you can automate the process of checking profile. Within 24 hours, eLink Pro can help you check about 800 profiles. However, eLink Pro does not guarantee that the profiles will do likewise. But this doesn't mean you won't have about 40 – 50 people checking your profile. And you can be sure that about 20-30 are likely to qualify as your leads.

eLink Pro is a simple way to enhance your marketing strategy. You have nothing to worry about building connections that make your profile standard, this tool makes it a little more effortless.

Crystal

Sometimes, there can be tools that pop up around a social media marketing tool. This is the kind of opportunity that you get when you take your chance with Crystal. Crystal is referred to the world's biggest personality network. When you have a premium account, you can get access to insight of the personality behind the account.

With the kind of information within your reach, striking a conversation with prospects will come easy for you. To a reasonable extent, you will be able to make a call and initiate a smart conversation with the person because you have a little knowledge about them.

It's recommended that you invest a great deal of effort into this because you might not really get something worthwhile to go with if you try to just compare a couple of LinkedIn profiles. But with Crystal, it becomes possible to see many areas that you can take advantage of.

Besides, this tool helps you to attain a more professional outlook as a marketer on LinkedIn. When you incorporate this into your marketing effort, it becomes easier to convert a shrugging connection to a significant lead.

LeadGrabber Pro

It's not enough to have just a lead, it's important that you have significant ones who can always be a guarantee of future patronage. Yet, you should know that this does not come easy. But don't worry, marketing tools like LeadGrabber Pro is your best bet.

It puts together a list of viable clients from popular networking sites such as LinkedIn. With this tool, you can assess some of the most important and faithful leads for your business. Also, it has the strength to get you email lists that can be used for your email marketing. If you are a B2B marketer, you shouldn't miss out on this tool.

Dux-Soup

Always, your business needs new leads if it must go from one level of growth to another. Dux-Soup makes that possible. This tool was designed majorly for LinkedIn users, so the category you belong to on the platform doesn't matter, this tool helps you to achieve your need for good relationship with connections.

Among other things, you can use it for your brand's visibility, generating of fresh leads, profile development for sales and marketing, and so on.

With this kind of tool, you can have free time to focus on other need for growth and expansion as far as your business is concerned.

LinkedIn Small Business

LinkedIn Small Business offers its users a three-way approach that places a business to strategically gain trust, increase sales, and achieve other related goals. The approaches are broken down below:

- Build audience relationship.
- Promote the presence of your brand.
- Engage them through content marketing.

The third approach is important to marketers as it helps them to give value to their audience. You should know that the right content helps you to attract the right audience. What's more? You can help them build the courage which they need to be in charge of their own decisions.

There are more than enough to even learn with this tool, so prepare your mind to spend good time learning all you can. You never can tell, you can come across the right strategy for reaching your targets on time.

LeadFuze

There are a lot of things to gain by staying visible on LinkedIn. Yet, despite a knowledge of this benefit, quite a lot of people still find the platform of about 610 million users complicated.

One of the challenges is comprehending the overwhelming data that is available on the platform. Even a lot of sales professional are having a difficult time processing the presence of over 610 million users. And this is where LeadFuze comes handy. This tool is important if you are interested in boosting your marketing strategy. With this tool, it becomes easy to generate a good number of targets and potential leads when you execute searches.

Unlike any other tool you can find, those who use this tool have access to phone numbers and email address, thereby making it possible to execute sales with less effort.

There is more. You also get to send follow-ups and emails within a short period of time because the process can be automated. Presently, it's possible to get data related to about 200 million premium accounts and B2B professionals. Plus, you won't have a problem gathering leads as about 350,000 prospects put up monthly.

Outro

If you want to discover potential clients using more than one source. It provides you with the following:

- The Outro community
- Your Network

It could be daunting going through a huge list of premium accounts from the search result only to realize that none is a potential lead. The case is different with Outro.

Outro helps you to avoid wasting limited time. Hence, you are able to carry out effective research. Using what it calls *relationship strength algorithm*, it executes other functions following a single request. The other features which you can optimize are:

- Developing reports using alternative.
- Exportation of data of contacts.
- CRM Incorporation.

As you can see, Outro is a resourceful tool. Using effective and efficient algorithmically driven process, it becomes easier to grow your network and identify qualified prospects.

Salestools.io

Salestools.io is another resources that you can use for lead generation on LinkedIn. Using a different approach, it allows users to export a list of leads from LinkedIn to excel. If you have the intent of tracking leads, this is the right tool for you.

It is very rare to find a tool that lets you download data directly to Excel, so if you find this kind of tool as a marketer, you shouldn't hesitate.

But that's not all. After having the list of prospects, you should take action by sending an email to them. Nothing to worry about too, this tool comes with a feature that makes it possible to send personalized email to every prospect. The feature is called sequence.

Salestools.io also makes it possible to keep track of your activities. This also means an opportunity to stay in control of leading prospects through how they process your sales funnel to your advantage.

It's one of the most advanced tool that you can use to improve the game of your marketing. We should however warn you that it is not a superb option if you are looking at skyrocketing your sales on LinkedIn.

Discoverly

Earlier, we recommended that you should build strong relationship with your connects by seeking them on other social media platforms. Well, the advice is still the same but this tool makes it easier for you.

When you use Discoverly, not only do you get necessary information about their LinkedIn profile, you will also get necessary data from other social media platform you also belong to. For instance, Discoverly can notify you if you share a mutual friend with your potential prospect on Facebook.

Since sales is about forging connection with significant leads, Discoverly makes it easier to gather different data from different platforms.

Please note that it's required that you use Chrome browser to access the internet in order to make use of Discoverly.

Rapportive

You have a Gmail account? If your answer is yes, you should get ready to optimize your account. Do you know that you can use your inbox as a tool for LinkedIn sales? All you have to do is get the Rapportive, a tool offered by Gmail. Once you install the free add-on for Firefox or Chrome, you can get the data you need about your contact delivered right into your inbox.

Thus, you don't have to be moving from one tab to the other.

For example, should you get an email from a contact who is interested in transacting with you, Rapportive has the capacity to supply you with the following:

- Location
- Mutual connection

- LinkedIn profile including the name and title of company.

LinkedIn Elevate

If you want to boost your reach and increase the chance of having your messages noticed, you need to create the right content. Not only that, you must use social media effectively in sharing your content.

By using LinkedIn Elevate, it has become very easy to share content. This app can work for desktop and mobile devices. Using its algorithm, LinkedIn Elevate scans its news sources and suggests articles that you can share on your profile.

Isn't it amazing that you can spend your time doing other things while you let LinkedIn Elevate take care of discovering and sharing of content related to your profile.

Guru

Whether you are working as an individual or within a network of sales and marketing team, it is important that you act smartly. That's where Guru comes in.

The need to boost sales means you will have to spend quality time checking profiles and different pages that belong to companies. And it doesn't just stop there, you have to make sense of the information you come across.

When you incorporate Guru into your marketing strategy, you can do the following with the information you come across:

- Know active users working in the same industry with you.
- Possible competitors.
- Sales that related to the prospect's industry.

Within a short period of time, Guru helps you find a good number if prospects. You commit no crime when you let Guru direct you to the leads within your reach within the same space. And if you are working as part of a team, you have many tools which you can use in distributing available information.

SalesLoft

Being in control of your business is a thing of joy. But you have a lot of work today especially with respect to generating sales and managing it constantly. To a very impressive extent, SalesLoft helps you to oversee the process of sales engagement. Without taking too much of your time, you get to establish a good bridge between yourself and your customers.

f you want to build real business connection through personalized marketing strategy, and having data-driven results to show for it, you should invest in this tool.

Voogy

This used to be known as Salestool.io. Voogy is an automatic marketing tool which is driven by the need to improve business strategy especially in respect to inbound and outbound engagement.

It's not enough to use any of the tools introduced to you without being able to grow and nurture your leads. So, this automated marketing tool is yours grab. Don't hesitate.

LinkedIn Marketing Tools: Making Use of the Best Option(s)

Once again, there are about 610 million users on LinkedIn. To reach your market niche among them, it's important that you use the right marketing tool. Not only that, you need to use it well too.

Among other things, the tools which have been introduced to you can ensure lead generation and good audience engagement with your content in order have good results to show. You should also know that each of the tools are unique and can be useful for the fulfilment of your business goals. They make your business strategy easier than you can ever imagine.

Using Tools Appropriately

You can trust LinkedIn marketing tools to deliver awesome results if you use them the right way. Remember that you need to use these tools in obedience to the policies of LinkedIn so as not to get banned or restricted on the platform.

What should you do to be safe? It is advised that you estimate your LinkedIn Range (LR). The range is 3.5-55% of your entire connections.

Take for example, if you have 5000 contacts, your LR will be about 150 – 250. Then, your limit of profile viewing will not be more than 500 if you are using LinkedIn Sales Navigator. To be realistic, most users will have a few connections and their LR may not be that high to fill the range.

Using LinkedIn Tools To Build Compound Connection

To use LinkedIn tools in building compound connection, you need to set a figure that is not outside your LR. If for instance you have 2,500 connections, your LR should be set within 100 – 150 limit of new connections each day.

Without having to send invitation to connect, you can also set your profile visits to 100–150. And naturally, a good number of contacts will also go through your profile thinking they are returning you a favour and in the process, they end up sending your connection request.

Mind you, you need to be active on LinkedIn in order to optimize your account. You can enhance your visibility by sharing content, liking the content of your connect; and uploading real content. When you are visible, you also get invitations to connect.

However, it is more important that you establish your LinkedIn limit while doing these things. You don't want to be banned or restricted for going beyond your limits.

Being Permanently Restricted Is Rare but Beware

Out of fear of being banned, some users do less on their profile. In fact, it was believed at some point that an update to the platform was aimed a particular automation tool.

And the truth is that LinkedIn keeps changing and improving. Constantly, the algorithm is improved on to enable its success.

On the other hand, the companies who are in the business of providing tools and apps for effective marketing on LinkedIn are also in the race of meeting up and breaking the standard each time there is an update. It is for this reason that about three most successful tools for LinkedIn automation in Chrome boasts of about 100,000 downloads.

Approved In-house Practices for LinkedIn Tools

Automation tools makes marketing operations on LinkedIn easy but staying in line with the best practices is important. Like a house which you must tidy up, you should make it a priority to attend to connection request. If you don't want to accept any invite, you shouldn't delay in rejecting it.

And then, you should get rid of pending requests. If you have pending requests, it's a red flag that notifies LinkedIn that you are trying to connect with those who don't know you.

So, to stay safe, you should get rid of unaccepted connection requests. Generally, if you are highly targeted in the LinkedIn growth strategy, your requests will be less outstanding.

Effective Tools Act Like the Real User

Automated tools can act like the real user on LinkedIn. But to stay safe, you need to set LR limit.

While using automation tools, you need to still be in charge. So, make sure you look for features like go/pause/stop. With these features, you can set up limits and make the tool do what you would be.

You don't want to risk being restricted if your automation tool is still at work by 2am. That time, you are probably asleep.

Tools Don't Offer the Same Functionalities

Software programs, browser extensions, plug-ins, third- party features, and bots are range of tools that you can find in software programs. But you need to verify that you have the tool that is necessary to getting your work done.

First, not all marketing tools have the same functionalities. Check the track record of the brains behind the tools/apps. Before you settle to any, ask yourself the questions below:

- What customer support do they support?
- How accessible can they be?
- Is it possible to speak to interact with the brains behind the tools/apps?

We recommend that you evaluate any marketing tool before you settle down to it so that you won't be shocked when your tool suddenly disappears. While you might come across a new tool that will beat an old one, it is highly recommended that you stick with the ones that have been in the market for so long. You can bet that it is the integrity of the tool that has so far sustained it.

Look out for testimonials. Look for how other companies who are using the LinkedIn tools similar to yours are thriving.

Be Resourceful

Don't just stop at using automation tools for your LinkedIn marketing strategy. You should be resourceful to your connections – share valuable content with them, update job opportunities, among others.

Before you take up any marketing tool, you should first establish the values you want to give. Once you have set the values you want to distribute, it will be easy to automate a marketing tool to execute it.

Now, some of the best practices you should consider when using tools are:

That being said, let's take a look at some of the best practices to consider when using a tool.

- Be careful before incorporating any tool
- Set your goals, your targets, and the things that will stimulate their interests.
- Obey the LinkedIn range limit.

- Be visible and targeted. The reward is great.
- Personalize messages and interactions. The reward is great.
- Set a goal for the extra time which you recover from using automated tools.

Circumventing LinkedIn Usage Limits

For a good navigation on LinkedIn, there are connection tools that can help you. Let's call them workarounds. With thoroughly designed workarounds, it is possible to find your way on LinkedIn without having worries about LinkedIn limit.

What's more? Using this approach doesn't affect your LinkedIn connection limit in any way. This is really an amazing option if you can't afford to pay for a premium account.

When Tools On LinkedIn Is Not Necessary

Despite talking about the great opportunities which LinkedIn offers, you should know that there are times when you don't need to use automated tools.

Whether you need an automation tool or not depends on the category of audience you are targeting. For example, a business CEO is not likely to accept request to connect from an individual than he would be willing to accept a request from another CEO.

Also, you should understand that sending using automation to send too many connection requests at a time on LinkedIn may not be an appropriate decision.

Conclusion

Wow! You have taken your time to read this guide to the end. It shows that you are really interested in learning all the details and resources that LinkedIn provides. I can bet you are now ready to incorporate LinkedIn into your marketing strategy. If you are still in doubt, I hope you understand you are letting a huge opportunity pass you by.

Be reminded again that you can never the kind of professional connections which LinkedIn offers on any other social media platform. Talk about lead generation and converting them to buyers, LinkedIn is an excellent platform.

Don't forget all the steps examined in this book. They are your ultimate guide to optimizing your presence online whether as an individual of business. Be customer-focused when executing your content creation plan. You need do build your brand around the targets if you want your sales effort to show measurable results.

Never stop giving value if you want your connections to trust you. Be visible, give value, share opportunities with your connections, and stay active. You shouldn't be active for some days only to be nowhere-to-be-found for another month. It's not important that you post every hour of the day. Incorporate media files into your content marketing. Beyond creating relevant content, add aesthetic values too by using images, animations, GIF, and infographics.

Then, you can use LinkedIn ads to boost your level of reach and sales.

It is recommended that you follow this guide with all diligence. And who knows, you might be able to use it to provide solutions to others who are yet to optimize their LinkedIn account. All of these tips and many more have been covered in this book, and will surely help you grow. And when you become an expert at incorporating LinkedIn marketing tools and are able to show good results, people can begin to come to you for services.

Above all, don't forget the need to learn patience. Growing your LinkedIn profile is not by magic. You can't get your significant leads overnight and it's not possible to get all the connections you are targeting at once. It takes times. Just don't forget to execute the strategies you have been introduced to in this book.

A lot of possibilities await you.

Good luck!

Bibliographies

LinkedIn Claims Half a Billion Users. (2019). Retrieved from
http://fortune.com/2017/04/24/linkedin-users/

Cooper, P. (2019). 16 LinkedIn Statistics That Matter to Marketers in 2019. Retrieved from
https://blog.hootsuite.com/linkedin-statistics-business/

Yurieff, K. (2019). Facebook hits 2 billion monthly users. Retrieved from
https://money.cnn.com/2017/06/27/technology/facebook-2-billion-users/index.html

The Global Trends That Will Shape Recruiting In 2015 [INFOGRAPHIC]. (2014). Retrieved from http://talent.linkedin.com/blog/index.php/2014/11/the-global-trends-that-will-shape-recruiting-in-2015

Tiwari, S. (2019). Importance of LinkedIn Marketing - Parangat's Blog. Retrieved from
https://www.parangat.com/blog/importance-of-linkedin-marketing/

[INFOGRAPHIC] Q2 2013: The State of LinkedIn. (2019). Retrieved from
http://blog.wishpond.com/post/54116170504/infographic-q2-2013-the-state-of-linkedin

The Sophisticated Guide to Marketing on LinkedIn. (2019). Retrieved from
https://business.linkedin.com/marketing-solutions/c/14/1/sophisticated-guide-for-marketing

DeMers, J. 10 Reasons Your Brand Needs To Be On LinkedIn. Retrieved from
https://www.forbes.com/sites/jaysondemers/2015/07/22/10-reasons-your-brand-needs-to-be-on-linkedin/#67bb48a23aca

Tiwari, S. (2019). Importance of LinkedIn Marketing - Parangat's Blog. Retrieved from
https://www.parangat.com/blog/importance-of-linkedin-marketing/

Osman, M. (2019). Mind-Blowing LinkedIn Statistics and Facts (2019). Retrieved from
https://kinsta.com/blog/linkedin-statistics/

The Deep Disconnect: An HR Data Report. Retrieved from https://getbambu.com/data-reports/deep-disconnect-hr-report/

14 LinkedIn Hacks That Will Triple the Size of Your Network in Two Weeks. (2017). Retrieved from https://blog.crazyegg.com/2016/08/29/14-linkedin-hacks-triple-network/

York, A. (2019). 5 LinkedIn Best Practices for Marketing Professionals. Retrieved from
https://sproutsocial.com/insights/linkedin-best-practices/

Walters, L. (2015). 10 statistics that show video is the future of marketing | MWP Digital Media. Retrieved from https://mwpdigitalmedia.com/blog/10-statistics-that-show-video-is-the-future-of-marketing/

Lloyd, D. (2015). SEO for Success in Video Marketing | Adobe Blog. Retrieved from https://theblog.adobe.com/seo-for-success-in-video-marketing/

Nguyen, C. (2015). 12 Webinar Stats You Need to Know. Retrieved from https://www.readytalk.com/blog/christine-nguyen/12-webinar-stats-you-need-to-know

Gibbs, A. (2019). How to Start a Podcast for Your Company. Retrieved from https://blog.spinweb.net/facts-about-business-podcasting-that-will-blow-your-mind

www.ingramcontent.com/pod-product-compliance
Lightning Source LLC
Chambersburg PA
CBHW020551220526
45463CB00006B/2260